SHAMBHALA
CLASSICS

NARROW ROAD
to the INTERIOR
and other writings

Matsuo Bashō

TRANSLATED FROM THE JAPANESE *by*

SAM HAMILL

SHAMBHALA
BOULDER
2000

Shambhala Publications, Inc.
4720 Walnut Street
Boulder, Colorado 80301
www.shambhala.com

14 13 12 11 10

Printed in the United States of America

⊗ This edition is printed on acid-free paper that meets the
American National Standards Institute z39.48 Standard.

♻ Shambhala Publications makes every effort to print on recycled paper.
For more information please visit www.shambhala.com.

Distributed in the United States by Penguin Random House LLC and
in Canada by Random House of Canada Ltd

Library of Congress Cataloging-in-Publication Data
Matsuo, Bashō, 1644–1694.
Narrow road to the interior: and other writings/Matsuo Bashō;
translated from the Japanese by Sam Hamill.
p.   cm.—(Shambhala classics)
Previous ed.: The essential Bashō, 1999.
Includes bibliographical references.
Contents: Narrow road to the interior—Travelogue of weather-beaten
bones—The knapsack notebook—Sarashina travelogue—Selected haiku.
ISBN 978-1-57062-716-3 (pbk.: alk. paper)
1. Matsuo, Bashō, 1644–1694—Translations into English. I. Matsuo,
Bashō, 1644–1694 Essential Bashō. II. Hamill, Sam. III. Title. IV. Series.
PL794.4.A24   2000
895.6'132—dc21
00-038786

To Gray Foster and Eron Hamill

And to Bill O'Daly, Galen Garwood, Keida Yusuke,
Christopher Yohmei Blasdel, and Peter Turner

Companions along the Way

CONTENTS

TRANSLATOR'S INTRODUCTION

The moon and sun are eternal travelers. Even the years wander on.
A lifetime adrift in a boat or in old age leading a tired horse into the
years, every day is a journey, and the journey itself is home.
                    —*Bashō: Oku-no-hosomichi*

B ASHŌ ROSE LONG BEFORE DAWN, but even at such an early
hour, he knew the day would grow rosy bright. It was spring,
1689. In Ueno and Yanaka, cherry trees were in full blossom, and
hundreds of families would soon be strolling under their branches,
lovers walking and speaking softly or not at all. But it wasn't cherry
blossoms that occupied his mind. He had long dreamed of crossing the
Shirakawa Barrier into the mountainous heartlands of northern Hon-
shu, the country called Oku—"the interior"—lying immediately to
the north of the city of Sendai. He patched his old cotton trousers and
repaired his straw hat. He placed his old thatched-roof hut in anoth-
er's care and moved several hundred feet down the road to the home
of his disciple-patron, Mr. Sampu, making final preparations before
embarkation.

   On the morning of May 16, dawn rose through a shimmering
mist, Mount Fuji faintly visible on the horizon. It was the beginning
of the Genroku period, a time of relative peace under the Tokugawa

shogunate. But travel is always dangerous. A devotee as well as a traveling companion, Bashō's friend, Sora, would shave his head and don the robes of a Zen monk, a tactic that often proved helpful at well-guarded checkpoints. Bashō had done so himself on previous journeys. Because of poor health, Bashō carried extra nightwear in his pack along with his cotton robe or *yukata*, a raincoat, calligraphy supplies, and of course *hanamuke*, departure gifts from well-wishers, gifts he found impossible to leave behind.

Bashō himself would leave behind a number of gifts upon his death some five years later, among them a journal composed after this journey, his health again in decline, a journal made up in part of fiction or fancy. But during the spring and summer of 1689, he walked and watched. And from early 1690 into 1694, Bashō wrote and revised his "travel diary," which is not a diary at all. *Oku* means "within" and "farthest" or "dead-end" place; *hosomichi* means "path" or "narrow road." The *no* is prepositional. *Oku-no-hosomichi*: the narrow road within; the narrow way through the interior. Bashō draws *Oku* from the place of that name located between Miyagino and Matsushima, but it is a name that inspires plurisignation.

Narrow Road to the Interior is much, much more than a poetic travel journal. Its form, *haibun*, combines short prose passages with haiku. But the heart and mind of this little book, its *kokoro*, cannot be found simply by defining form. Bashō completely redefined haiku and transformed *haibun*. These accomplishments grew out of arduous studies in poetry, Buddhism, history, Taoism, Confucianism, Shintoism, and some very important Zen training.

Bashō was a student of Saigyō, a Buddhist monk-poet who lived five hundred years earlier (1118–1190), and who is the most prominent poet of the imperial anthology, *Shinkokinshū*. Like Saigyō before him, Bashō believed in co-dependent origination, a Buddhist idea holding that all things are fully interdependent, even at point of origin; that no thing is or can be completely self-originating. Bashō said of Saigyō, "He was obedient to and at one with nature and the four seasons." The *Samantabhadra-bodhisattva-sutra* says, "Of one thing it is said, 'This is good,' and of another it is said, 'This is bad,' but there is nothing inherent in either to make them 'good' or 'bad.' The 'self' is empty of independent existence." From Saigyō, the poet learned the importance of "being at one with nature," and the relative unimportance of mere personality. Such an attitude creates the Zen broth in which his poetry is steeped. Dreaming of the full moon as it rises over boats at Shiogama Beach, Bashō is not looking outside himself—rather he is seeking that which is most clearly meaningful within, and locating the "meaning" within the context of juxtaposed images that are interpenetrating and interdependent. The images arise naturally out of the *kokoro*—the heart/mind, as much felt as perceived.

Two hundred years earlier, Komparu Zenchiku wrote, "The Wheel of Emptiness is the highest level of art of the Noh—the performance is *mushin*." This is the art of artlessness, the act of composition achieved without "sensibility" or style—this directness of emotion expressed without ornament set the standards of the day.

At the time of the compiling of the *Man'yōshū*, the first imperial anthology, completed in the late eighth century, the Japanese critical vocabulary emphasized two aspects of the poem: *kokoro*, which included sincerity, conviction, or "heart"; and also "craft" in a most particular way. *Man'yōshū* poets were admired for their "masculinity," that is, for uncluttered, direct, and often severe expression of emotion. Their sincerity (*makoto*) was a quality to be revered. The poets of the *Man'yōshū* are the foundation upon which all Japanese poetry has been built.

One of the first *karon*, or essays on literary criticism in Japanese, is that of Fujiwara Hamanari (733–799), author of *Kakyō-hyōshiki*, an essay listing seven "diseases of poetry," such as having the first and second lines end on the same syllable, or having the last syllable of the third and last lines differ. There were various dissertations on "poem diseases," all largely modeled on the original Chinese of Shen Yo (441–513). The idea of studying craft in poetry must have caught on quickly, because by 885 the first *uta-awase*, or poetry-writing contests, were being held and were judged by guidelines drawn from these various essays on prosody.

At the time of the compilation of the *Man'yōshū*, very little poetry was being written in Chinese; Hitomaro and Yakamochi, the great eighth-century poets, wrote without many allusions to Confucian or Buddhist classics, their poems drawing inspiration from landscape and experience that are uniquely Japanese. Another court anthology contemporary with the *Man'yōshū*, the *Kaifusō*, represents the introduction of poetry written in Chinese language and styles, despite the few samples in the *Man'yōshū*.

Through the influence of the monk Kūkai, also called Kōbō Daishi (774–835), the study of Chinese became the norm for what amounted to a Buddhist aristocracy. As founder of the Shingon or True Word sect in Japan, Kūkai followed a tradition of secret oral teachings passed on from master to disciple, and had himself spent two years studying in China under Hui Kuo (764–805). The later influence of Sugawara-no-Michizane established Chinese as the language of scholarly poets, so much so that upon his death, Michizane was enshrined as a god of literature and calligraphy. His followers found Japanese forms too restrictive for their multilayered poetry. Every good poet was a teacher of poetry in one way or another, many taking on disciples. Michizane's influence was profound. He advocated both rigorous scholarship and genuine sincerity in composition; his own verses were substantially influenced by the T'ang dynasty poet Po Chü-i. The form was *shih*, lyric verse composed in five- or seven-character lines written in Chinese; but, unlike most earlier Japanese poets, Michizane wrote poems that were deceptively simple and, like the poetry of Po Chü-i, strengthened by a combination of poignancy and conviction. Poetry written in Chinese was called *kanshi*, and Michizane established it as a major force.

In his *kana* (phonetic syllabary) preface to the *Kokinshū* in the tenth century, Ki-no-Tsurayuki, author of the famous travelogue *Tosa Journal*, lists six types of poetry:

1. soe-uta: suggestive or indirect expression of feeling
2. kazoe-uta: clear, direct expression of feeling
3. nazurae-uta: parabolic expression
4. tatoe-uta: expression that conceals powerful emotion
5. tadagoto-uta: refinement of a traditional expression
6. iwai-uta: poem expressing congratulations or praise

Tsurayuki's list owes something to Lu Chi's catalogue of genres in his third-century Chinese *Art of Writing* (*Wen Fu*), which is itself indebted to various treatises on the Confucian poetry anthology, *Shih Ching* or *Poetry Classic*.

Much of the penchant for cataloguing and classifying types of poetry is the result of the Confucian classic, *Ta Hsueh* or *Great Learning*, in which Confucius says, "All wisdom is rooted in learning to call things by the right name," and that when "things are properly identified, they fall into natural categories and understanding [and, consequently, *action*] becomes orderly." Lu Chi, the dedicated student of Confucius, reminds us that the art of letters has "saved governments from certain ruin," and "clarifies laws" of nature and society. He finds within the study of writing itself a way to set his own life in order.

Such thinking undoubtedly lies behind Bashō's notion of the Way of Poetry.

Studying Chinese, the Japanese literati picked up Lu Chi's habit of discussing poetry in terms of form and content. And from the fifth-century Chinese scholar, Liu Hsieh, they drew the term *amari-no-kokoro*, a translation of Liu's original *yu wei* or "aftertaste." As a critical term, it would be used and reshaped and used again; it is still a part of literary evaluation in the late twentieth century. Narihira says of a poem in the *Kokinshū*, "*Kokoro amarite—kotoba tarazu*," or "Plenty of heart; not enough words." Kuronushi says, "*Kokoro okashikute, sama iyashi*," or "Interesting *kokoro*, but a rather common form." The poet strives for the quality called *amari-no-kokoro*, meaning that the heart/soul of the poem must reach far beyond the words themselves, leaving an indelible aftertaste.

For Bashō, this most often meant a resonance found in nature. When he invokes the call of a cuckoo, its very name, *hototogisu* (pronounced with a virtually silent closing vowel), invokes its lonely cry. Things are as they are. Insight permits him to perceive a natural poignancy in the beauty of temporal things—*mono-no-aware*—and cultivate its expression into great art. *Aware* originally meant simply emotion initiated by engagement of the senses. In its own way, this phrase is Japan's equivalent of William Carlos Williams's dictum, "No ideas but in things."

In *The World of the Shining Prince*, Ivan Morris's study of *The Tale of Genji*, Morris says of *aware*:

> In its widest sense it was an interjection or adjective refer-
> ring to the emotional quality inherent in objects, people,
> nature, and art, and by extension it applied to a person's
> internal response to emotional aspects of the external

world. . . . In Murasaki's time [c. 1000 CE] *aware* still retained its early catholic range, its most characteristic use in *The Tale of Genji* is to suggest the pathos inherent in the beauty of the outer world, a beauty that is inexorably fated to disappear together with the observer. Buddhist doctrines about the evanescence of all living things naturally influenced this particular content of the word, but the stress in *aware* was always on direct emotional experience rather than on religious understanding. *Aware* never entirely lost its simple interjectional sense of "Ah!"

As a more purely critical term in later centuries, *aware* identified a particular quality of elegant sadness, a poignant awareness of temporality, a quality found in abundance, for instance, in the poetry of Issa and in this century in the novels of Kawabata Yasunari. Middle-aged and in declining health, Bashō found plenty of resonance in temporal life, much of it clarified through his deep study of the classics.

Tsurayuki, whose own diary provided a model for Bashō's travelogues 700 years later, ruminated on the art of letters during his sojourn through Tosa province in the south of Shikoku Island in 936. In his preface to the *Kokinshū*, he lists several sources for inspiration in poetry, all melancholy in one way or another: "Looking at falling blossoms on a spring morning; sighing over snows and waves which reflect the passing years; remembering a fall from fortune into loneliness." Tsurayuki's proclivity for melancholy perhaps explains the general tone of the *Kokinshū*. But this, too, is *mono-no-aware*.

At the time of the *Man'yōshū*, Zen was being brought to Japan via a steady stream of scholars returning from China. Along with Zen equations and conversations, the scholars also brought with them Chinese poetics, including a surprising Confucian faith in the power of the right word rightly used. The attitude is paradoxical: the Zen poet believes the real experience of poetry lies somewhere beyond the words themselves but, like a good Confucian, believes simultaneously that only the perfect word perfectly placed has the power to reveal the authentic experience of the poem.

Ki-no-Tsurayuki's co-compiler of the *Kokinshū*, Mibu-no-Tada-mine (868–965), introduced another new term to the Japanese critical canon by praising a quality in certain poems which he called *yūgen*, a word borrowed from Chinese Buddhist writing to identify "depth of meaning," a character made by combining the character for "dim" or "dark" with the character identifying a deep, reddish black color. Tadamine used *yūgen* to identify "aesthetic feeling *not explicitly expressed*." He wanted a term by which to identify subtleties and implications. Over the course of the next hundred or so years, *yūgen* would also be adopted by Zennists to define "ghostly qualities," as in ink paintings. But the term's origin lies within seventh-century Chinese Buddhist literary terminology. As an aesthetic concept, it was esteemed throughout the medieval period. An excellent study of Buddhism and literary arts in medieval Japan, William R. LaFleur's *The Karma of Words*, devotes an entire chapter to *yūgen*.

The compilation of the *Kokinshū* also institutionalized the *makura kotoba*, or "pillow word," in Japanese poetics. It is a fixed epithet, often like Homer's "wine-dark sea," but frequently allowing for double entendre or multiple evocation. Although such devices appear infrequently in the *Man'yōshū*, by the time of the *Kokinshū*, most readers were aware that "clouds and rain" might mean sexual congress as well as weather patterns. The *makura kotoba* often permitted a poet to disguise emotions; it was both "polite" and metaphoric.

Along with the pillow word, the apprentice poet also learned how to make use of the *kake kotoba* or "pivot word" that would later become central to the composition of haiku. It is a play on different meanings of a word that links two phrases. It is often nearly impossible to translate except when it creates an intentional pause. The pivot word creates deliberate ambiguity, often implying polysignation. The pillow word and the pivot word have been reassessed and discussed and reexamined throughout the history of Japanese poetry.

As this critical vocabulary developed, poets devised new ways to discuss the *kajitsu* or formal aspects of a poem. The *ka* is the "beautiful surface of the poem," and the *jitsu* is the "substantial core." Studying the "beautiful surface" of the poem along with its interior structure, Fujiwara-no-Kinto (966–1041) composed his *Nine Steps of Waka* (waka is a generic term for classical poems of five lines measured in syllabic lines of 5-7-5-7-7) to establish standards based almost solely on critical fashion. Certain rhymes were taboo at a poem's closure; certain vowel sounds should be repeated at particular intervals. Rather than being a general and moral and emotional discourse such as Lu Chi's, or those of Tsurayuki and Tadamine, Kinto's aesthetic relied exclusively on reasoned study of the architecture of the poem. His critical vocabulary is restricted to that of the poem's structure. His anthology, *Shuishū*, has never enjoyed either the popularity or the controversy of the *Kokinshū* and *Shinkokinshū*.

Zen demolishes much of this kind of literary criticism by pointing out that, seen from the core, the surface is very deep; inasmuch as cause leads to effect, effect in turn produces cause. A poem's "depth" cannot be created by packing the poem with allusions and implications—hermetics alone. Still, *surface* and *core* may be useful terms for establishing a necessary dialectic; they provide frames of reference. Such discussions of depths and surfaces certainly contributed to Bashō's critical vocabulary and to his notion of the Way of Elegance in poetry.

As this critical vocabulary came into use, it was balanced by a vocabulary of the emotions. A contemporary of Saigyō, Fujiwara Teika (1162–1241), attacked structural criticism as hopelessly inadequate. "Every poem," he said, "must have *kokoro*. A poem without *kokoro* is not—cannot be—a true poem; it is only an intellectual exercise." Thus, by combining a vocabulary for the apparatus of poetry with a vocabulary for the emotional states of poetry, Teika believed, a poem could be examined and properly appreciated. His insistence on the true poem's *kokoro* returns the experience of the poem to human dimensions.

Another term in use at the time, *kokai*, expressed a feeling of regret after reading a poem, a consequence of the poet having failed to think sufficiently deeply prior to its composition. It was a criticism not often applied to Bashō, nor to other poets working in the Zen tradition, but one with which every haiku poet since has struggled. Bashō sought a natural spontaneity, a poetry that would indulge no regrets of any kind. Zen discipline is built in part around the idea of truth articulated in spontaneous response. A "correct" response to a Zen koan, for instance, need not be obviously rational or logical. Bashō sought a poetry that was a natural outgrowth of being Bashō, of living in this world, of making the journey itself one's home.

The fourteenth-century Zen monk Ikkyū Sōjun wrote, "*Ame furaba fure, kaze fukaba fuke.*" If it rains, let it rain; if the wind blows, let it blow. Bashō spent many years struggling to "learn how to listen as things speak for themselves." No regrets. He refused to be anthropocentric. The theory of co-dependent origination infuses seer and seen, making them not two things, but one. Seeing the more than two hundred beautiful pine-covered islands off the coast of Matsushima, he wrote:

Matsushima ya

ah Matsushima ya

Matsushima ya

This is the sort of poem that can be done once, and once only. But it is quintessentially Bashō, both playful and inspired, yet with a hint of *mono-no-aware*, a trace of the pathos of beautiful mortality. A literal translation: "Pine Islands, ah! / Oh, Pine Islands, ah! / Pine Islands, ah!"

Simple as it is, the poem implies co-dependent origination, physical landscape, and a breathless—almost speechless—reverence. Just as Bashō learned utterly direct simplicity from Ikkyū, he learned from Ikkyū's friend, Rikyū, that each tea ceremony is the only tea ceremony. Therefore, each poem is the only poem. Each moment is the only moment in which one can be fully aware. Standing on the shore, he saw hundreds of tiny islands carved by tides, wind-twisted pines rising at sharp angles. *Matsu* means pine; *shima* is island. *Ya* indicates subject, but also works simultaneously as an exclamation. It functions as a *kireji* or "cutting word." The township on the mainland is itself called Matsushima. Bashō entered Matsushima by boat in June 1689 and was so taken by its beauty that he declared it to have been made by Oyama-zumi, god of the mountains.

Bashō walked and dreamed along the beach at Ojima beneath the moon of Matsushima. From his pack, he withdrew a poem written by a friend and former teacher, Sodō, an acknowledged haiku master. The poem described Matsushima and was written in Chinese. Another, a poem in Japanese about Matsugaura-shima, was composed by an Edo doctor, Hara Anteki. The poems, Bashō said, were his companions during a long sleepless night.

Two days later, he visited an elegant temple, Zuigan-ji, founded thirty-two generations earlier by Makabe-no-Heishiro upon his return from a decade of studies in China. Bashō wondered whether it might be "the gates of buddha-land." But he was no flower child wandering in Lotus Land. His journey is a pilgrimage; it is a journey into the interior of the self as much as a travelogue, a vision quest that concludes in insight. But there is no conclusion. The journey itself is home. The means is the end, just as it is the beginning. Each step is the first step, each step the last.

Bashō visited temples only in part because he was himself a Zennist. Temples often provided rooms for wayfarers, and the food, if simple, was good. The conversation was of a kind the literate pilgrim especially enjoys. Bashō, among the most literate poets of his time, seems to be everywhere in the presence of history. Oku-no-hosomichi overflows with place names, famous scenes, literary Chinese and Buddhist allusions, and literary echoes called honkadori—borrowed or quoted lines and paraphrases. But he didn't stay at many temples during his most famous journey; he rarely stayed at inns; he was generally and generously entertained by local haikai poets and put up by wealthy families. His health failing and each year passing more quickly, he enjoyed his modest celebrity and its benefits.

His literary and spiritual lineage included Kamo-no-Chōmei (1154–1216), Shinkokinshū poet, author of the Mumyōshō, a kind of manual of writing, and of the Hōjōki, an account of Chōmei's years in a "ten-foot-square hut" following a series of calamities in Kyoto. Like Chōmei, Bashō, despite being deeply versed in Chinese and Japanese literature, philosophy, and history, enjoyed talking with working people everywhere. Besides being one of Bashō's models for travel writing, Chōmei was a model for the practice of compassion.

After "abandoning the world," Chōmei moved to the mountains on the outskirts of Kyoto. But his was not to be the usual life of the

Zen ascetic. He made very regular trips to town, if for no other reason than to listen to the people he met there. Reading the *Hōjōki*, it is easy to forget that Chōmei served as a kind of journalist, a deeply compassionate witness to the incredible suffering of people during his lifetime. His world was shaken to the core when winds spread a great fire through Kyoto, leveling a third of the capital city in 1177. In 1181, a famine began that lasted two years. These and other calamities informed Chōmei's understanding of the First Noble Truth, that "being is agonizing," and inspired his profound sense of compassion. Just as a disciple of Sakyamuni Buddha, Vimalakirti, provided a model for Chōmei's retreat, Bashō found in Chōmei a model for compassion-ate engagement with others. Chōmei had written, "Trivial things spo-ken along the way enliven the faith of my awakened heart."

Chōmei's interest in people in general was a trait Bashō shared. He also could not separate his life from his art. Bashō also felt a deep connection to history. He speaks as though all eternity were only yes-terday, each memory vivid, the historical figures themselves almost contemporaneous; he speaks confidentially, expecting his reader to be versed in details so that his own brief travelogue may serve to call up enormous resonances, ghosts at every turn. But Bashō doesn't pack his lines with references. His subjects and his knowledge flow freely, ca-sually, through his writing.

Chōmei bore witness to countless thousands of deaths after the great fire swept Kyōto: "They die in the morning and are born in the evening like bubbles on water." Bashō walks across the plain where a great battle once raged. Only empty fields remain. The landscape re-minds him of a poem by Tu Fu (712–770) in which the T'ang poet surveyed a similar scene and wrote,

> The whole country devastated,
> only mountains and rivers remain.

In springtime, at the ruined castle,
the grass is always green.

For Bashō, the grass blowing in the breeze seems especially poignant, so much so that his eyes fill with tears. If Tu Fu, both as a poet and as a man, is a fit model—to be emulated, not imitated, Bashō insists—he is reminded of how little we have learned from all our interminable warfare and bloodshed. The wind blows. The grasses bend. Bashō moistens his brush months later and writes, remembering,

Summer grasses—
all that remains of great soldiers'
imperial dreams.

Natsugusa ya
tsuwamono domo ga
yume no ato

His echo of Tu Fu underscores the profound irony. For Bashō, the journey into the interior of the way of poetry had been long and arduous. His simple "summer grasses" haiku carried within it the sort of resonance he sought throughout his life. The grasses with their plethora of associations, the ghosts of Hidehira, Yoritomo, and Yoshitsune, an allusion drawn from a famous Noh drama—Bashō framed his verse with rich and complex historical, literary, and philosophical associations. The poem implies that the grasses are the *only* consequence of warriors' dreams, that the grasses are all that remain of the immeasurable desires of all passing generations.

The haiku itself is spare, clean, swift as a boning knife. The melopoeia combines *a, o,* and *u* sounds: *tsu, gu* in line one; *tsu* and *yu* in lines two and three; the *tsu* sound is very quick. The *a* sound punctuates the whole poem: *na, sa, ya* among the five syllables of line one; *wa* and *ga* among the seven syllables of line two, the four remaining being *mono* and *domo*; and a semiconcluding *a* before *to*. Among the seventeen syllables are six *a* syllables, six *o* syllables, and four *u* syllables.

The Western reader, accustomed to being conscious of reading translation and having fallen into the unrewarding habit of reading poetry silently, often misses Bashō's ear by neglecting the *romaji* or romanized Japanese printed with the poems. Onomatopoeia, rhyme, and slant rhyme are Bashō's favorite tools, and he uses them like no one else in Japanese literature. He wrote from within the body; his poems are full of breath and sound as well as images and allusions.

What Bashō read, he read deeply and attentively. As a poet, he had blossomed slowly, ever changing, constantly learning. The poetry of his twenties and thirties is competent and generally undistinguished. It is the learned poetry of received ideas composed by a good mind. It lacks breadth and depth of vision.

As his interest in Chinese poetry continued to grow, he studied Tu Fu assiduously during his twenties and thirties, and he read Li Po for his rich imagination and inventive styles of writing. Foremost among his studies, he claimed to have "always traveled with a copy of *Chuang Tzu*." He seems to have struggled with Zen discipline and Chinese poetry and philosophy all during his thirties, and the result was a poetry at first clearly derivative, but later becoming ever more his own as he grew into his studies. Upon entering his forties, Bashō's verse began to change. He learned to be comfortable with his teachers and with his own scholarship. His Zen practice had steadied his vision. Fewer aspirations stood in his way.

Born in 1644 in Ueno, Iga Province, approximately thirty miles southeast of Kyoto, the son of Matsuo Yozaemon, a low-ranking samurai, Bashō had at least one elder brother and four sisters. As a young man, he served in the household of a high-ranking local samurai, Tōdō Shinshichiro, becoming a companion to his son, Yoshitada, whose "haiku name" was Sengin. Bashō often joined his master in composing the linked verses called *haikai no renku*, but was still known by his samurai name, Matsuo Munefusa, despite having taken his first haiku name, Sobo. Bashō also had a common-law wife at this time, Jutei, who later became a nun. And although there is little verifiable information on these years, he seems to have experimented a good deal. He would later say on reflection, "I at one time coveted an official post" and, "There was a time when I became fascinated with the ways of homosexual love."

Whether because of a complicated love-life or whether as a result of the death of his friend and master, Bashō apparently simply wandered off sometime around the beginning of 1667, leaving behind his samurai name and position. It was not unique for a man like Bashō to leave samurai society. Many who did so became monks. Most others entered the merchant class. Bashō, uniquely, did neither. Some early biographers claim he went to Kyoto to study philosophy, poetry, and calligraphy. In any event, he reemerged in 1672 as editor and commentator for a volume of *haikai*, *The Seashell Game* (Kai Oi). With contributions from about thirty poets, *The Seashell Game* shows Bashō to be witty, deeply knowledgeable, and rather lighthearted. It was well enough received to encourage him to move to Edo (present-day Tokyo).

While it is not clear whether he initially made his living in Edo working as a haiku poet and teacher, Bashō does tell us that those first years in the growing city were not easy ones. He would later recall that he was torn between the desire to become a great poet and the desire to give up verse altogether. But his verse was, in many ways, his life. He continued to study and write, and to attract students, a number of whom were, like himself, dropouts from samurai or *bushidō* society who also rejected the vulgar values of the class below the samurai, the *chonin* or urban merchant class. Bashō believed literature provided an alternative set of values, which he called *fūga-no-michi*, the "Way of Elegance." He claimed that his life was stitched together "by the single thread of art" which permitted him to follow "no religious law" and no popular customs.

He admired the Zen mind; but the "Buddhism" attached to Zen was, to him, almost superfluous. During his years in Edo, he studied Zen under the priest Butchō (1642–1715), apparently even to the point of considering the monastic life, but whether to escape from decadent culture or as a philosophical passion remains unclear. Despite his ability to attract students, he seems to have spent much of his time in a state of perpetual despondency, loneliness everywhere crowding in on him. No doubt this state of mind was compounded by chronically poor health, but Bashō was also engaging true *sabishi*, a spiritual loneliness that served *haikai* culture in much the same way *mu* or "nothingness" served Zen.

In the summer of 1676, Bashō visited his homeland for the first time since moving to Edo. Returning in late summer, he brought with him a nephew, Tōin, who was sixteen and who would remain in Bashō's care the remainder of his short life. Desperately in need of money to care for his nephew, the poet worked from 1677 to 1681 for a district waterworks company, while establishing a name in haiku contests and collaborating with other poets.

In the winter of 1680, his students built him a small hut on the east bank of the Sumida River, where he could establish a permanent home. In the spring, someone planted a plantain (or *bashō*) tree in the yard, giving the hut, "Bashō-an," its name, and the poet his final new nom de plume. He wrote, "After nine springs and autumns of living in poverty in the city, I have now moved to the Fukagawa district. Perhaps because I am poor, I remember the T'ang dynasty poet who observed, 'Chang-an (the Chinese capital) has always been a place for those seeking fame and fortune. But it's a tough place for the empty-handed wanderer.' "

The original Bashō-an burned to the ground when a fire swept through the neighborhood in the winter of 1682. Friends and disciples built a new one during the winter of 1683. His disciples were also beginning to earn names of their own. Bashō wrote of one, Kikaku, that his poems contained the "spiritual broth" of Tu Fu. But his followers were also time consuming. And there were suddenly second-generation disciples, literally hundreds of "Bashō group" poets springing up. More and more projects were offered for his possible participation. He longed for quietude. And he immersed himself in studying the Taoist masterpiece *Chuang Tzu*, and in his Zen studies under Butchō. Several of his poems from this period draw directly from Chuang Tzu's allegories, perhaps most obviously:

In this season's rain
the crane's long legs
have suddenly been shortened

Samidare ni
tsuru no ashi
mijikaku nareri

But for the "seasonal word," the poem is almost a quotation, and unusual for its syllabic structure of 5-5-7. He would later write to a disciple, "Even if you have three or four extra syllables, or even five or seven, you needn't worry as long as it *sounds* right. But if even one syllable is stale in your mouth, give it all of your attention."

The first full-length anthology of "Bashō school" haiku (*Minashi-guri*, or *Withered Chestnuts*) was published in the summer of 1683 with an afterword by Bashō in which he spells out the "four principal flavors" of the poems as the lyricism of Tu Fu and Li Po, the Zen of Han Shan, and the romantic love of Po Chu-i. He continues to find models and inspiration drawn from the T'ang dynasty poets.

During 1684 and early 1685, Bashō traveled to Kyoto, Nara, and his old home in Ueno, and composed *Travelogue of Weather-Beaten Bones* (*Nozaraishi Kikō*), the first of his travel journals and one notable for its undertone of pathos. His mother had died in Ueno the previous year, but Bashō had been too poor to be able to make the journey to her funeral.

He spent only a few days in Ueno, but his meeting with his brothers inspired one of his most famous poems:

If I took it in hand,
it would melt in my hot tears—
heavy autumn frost

Te ni toraba
kien namida so atsuki
aki no shimo

The trip was a long eight months, arduous and extremely dangerous. The forty-year-old poet had spent thirty years in Iga and a decade in Edo before beginning the wanderer's life for which he became so famous. This first travelogue reads almost as though it were translated from Chinese, allusions and parallels drawn from Ch'an (Zen) literature in nearly every line. Bashō was struggling to achieve a resonance between the fleeting moment and the eternal, between the instant of awareness and the vast emptiness of Zen.

In 1687, he traveled with his friend, Sora, and a Zen monk to Kashima Shrine, fifty miles east of Edo, where, among other things, Bashō visited his Zen master, Butchō, who had retired there. His record of this trip, *Kashima Travelogue,* is very brief, and the poems included are almost all by Bashō's disciples.

During his years of Zen training, he had spoken of striving to achieve the "religious flavor" of the poetry of Han Shan (*Kanzan* in Japanese, Cold Mountain in English); he had wanted to "clothe in Japanese language" the poetry of Po Chü-i. But in *Kashima Travelogue,* he chose a far simpler syntax, writing almost exclusively in *kana,* the Japanese phonetic syllabary, rather than in *kanji,* Chinese written characters. He was simplifying and clarifying his methods without sacrificing depth.

In late 1687, Bashō made another journey, visiting Ise, Nagoya, Iga, Yoshino, and Nara, traveling with a disciple and drinking companion, Etsujin. The writing from this journey would not be published until 1709, more than ten years after the poet's death. Scholars date completion of the *Knapsack Notebook* (*Oi-no-kobumi*) at about 1691, the same time the poet was writing *Oku-no-hosomichi.* Bashō attributes to his friend a great fondness for sake drinking and a splendid talent for singing ancient poetry to the accompaniment of the Japanese lute, or *biwa,* and records a number of parties held in their honor. Their travels through Ise, Yoshino, Suma, and Akashi resulted in some luminous haiku and some striking commentary on the Way of Poetry. He says in the *Knapsack* manucript, "Nobody has succeeded in making any improvement in travel diaries since Ki-no-Tsurayuki, Chōmei, and the nun Abutsu . . . the rest have merely imitated."

Clearly, he was searching for a style that could reinvigorate an ancient form. He must have felt he had gained a powerful knowledge that only a simple style could accommodate. He also said in *The Knapsack Notebook*, "Saigyō's *waka*, Sōgi's *renga*, / Sesshū's *sumi*, Rikyu's tea— the spirit which moves them is one spirit." But he was not filled with confidence, either, noting that all his attempts to reinvigorate the travelogue and to "become the equal" of Japan's greatest poets may amount to no more than "mere drunken chatter, the incoherent babbling of a dreamer." Nevertheless, he felt driven to take these risks, both physical and literary.

His next journal, *Sarashina Travelogue*, is the result of a short moonviewing trip Bashō had wanted to make to watch the moon rise through the trees over Mount Obasute. In a particularly poignant moment, offered a toast, he and his companions were given cups by the innkeeper, cups that caught his attention. Although cheap and gaudy, because of the locale, he found them to be "more precious than the blue jeweled cups of the wealthy."

After flirting with dense Chinese diction, Bashō was turning toward *wabi*, an elegant simplicity tinged with *sabi*, an undertone of "aloneness." *Sabi* comes from the purer "loneliness" of *sabishisa*. It was an idea that fit perfectly with his notion of *fuga-no-michi*, the Way of Elegance, together with his rejection of bourgeois values. Elegant simplicity. His idea of *sabi* has about it elements of *yūgen*, *mono-no-aware*, and plenty of *kokoro*. His poetry, so indebted to Japanese and Chinese classics, could be simplified; he could find a poetry that would instill in the reader a sense of *sabi*. Perhaps he had followed classical Chinese rhetorical conventions a bit too closely. He wanted to make images that positively radiated with reality.

Whether he had arrived at his mature style by that early spring morning in 1689, he was eager to begin his journey north to Sendai and on to Hiraizumi, where the Fujiwara clan had flourished and perished. He would then push west, cross the mountains, turn south down the west coast of Honshu along the Sea of Japan, then turn east again toward Ise, the vast majority of the trip to be made on foot. He left behind the idiosyncrasies and frivolities of the Teitoku and Danrin schools of *haikai*. He left perhaps as many as sixty advanced students of the Bashō school who, in turn, were acquiring students of their own.

When his disciple, Kikaku, overpraised a Bashō image of a cold fish on a fishmonger's shelf, saying he had attained "true mystery and depth," Bashō replied that what he most valued was the poem's "ordinariness." He had come almost full circle from the densely allusive Chinese style into a truly elegant simplicity that was in no way frivolous. He had elevated haiku from wordplay into powerful lyric poetry, from a game played by educated poetasters into a genuinely spiritual dimension. "Abide by rules," Bashō taught, "then throw them out!—only *then* may you achieve true freedom." His freedom expressed itself by redefining haiku as a complete form capable of handling complex data, emotional depth, and spiritual seriousness while still retaining some element of playfulness. R.H. Blyth wrote, "Zen is poetry; poetry is Zen." In the case of Bashō, the practice of Zen and the practice of poetry produce a seamless union.

Confucius says, "Only the one who attains perfect sincerity under heaven may discover one's 'true nature.' One who accomplishes this participates fully in the transformation of heaven and earth, and being fully human, becomes with them a third thing." Knowing this, Bashō tells his students, "Do not simply follow in the footsteps of the ancients; seek what they sought." To avoid simply filling the ancient footsteps of his predecessors, he studies them assiduously, attentively. And when he has had his fill of ancient poets and students and the infinite dialectic that is literature and art, when his heart is filled with wanderlust, he chooses a traveling companion, fills a small pack with essentials—and, of course, a few *hanamuke*—and walks off into the mid-May dawn, into the geography of the soul that makes the journey itself a home.

CHRONOLOGY

1644   Matsuo Bashō is born at or near Ueno in Iga Province, approximately thirty miles southeast of Kyoto.

1656   Bashō's father dies. Bashō enters the service of Tōdō Yoshitada, the son of a local high-ranking samurai.

1666   Yoshitada dies. Leaving the samurai family he has served, Bashō wanders, perhaps to Kyoto to study philosophy, poetry, and calligraphy.

1672   Moves to Edo in search of a new career. Studies Zen under priest Butchō (1642–1715). Edits a volume of *haikai*, *The Seashell Game*, with contributions by about thirty poets and commentary by Bashō.

1676   Briefly visits Ueno, his homeland.

1680   Bashō's students build him a small hut on the banks of the Sumida River.

1682   Bashō's hut is burned to the ground by fire. He takes refuge in Kai Province for a few months.

1683   *Withered Chestnuts*—the first full-length anthology of haiku by the "Bashō school"—is published, with an afterword by Bashō. His mother dies in Ueno. A new "Bashō hut" is built.

1684–85   Goes on the journey that results in *Travelogue of Weather-Beaten Bones*.

1687   Travels to Kashima and writes *A Visit to Kashima Shrine*. A trip to Sarashina results in *Sarashina Travelogue*. In the same year, he also takes a journey to Ise, Nagoya, Iga, Yoshino, and Nara; his record of this trip, *The Knapsack Notebook*, was published in 1709, ten years after the poet's death.

1689   Journeys through the northern provinces of Honshu, which provides the material for *Narrow Road to the Interior*, completed sometime later. Late in the year, Bashō returns to his hometown of Ueno.

1690   Visits friends and disciples in the Kyoto area. Visits the village of Zeze, on the shores of Lake Biwa, and stays for several months.

1692   Bashō moves into a new hut at the mouth of the Sumida River.

1693   Falls into a depression following the death of his nephew Tōin. In August, suffering from headaches and fever, Bashō bolts the gates to his hut, refusing to see anyone.

1694   With his mood lifted but his health still frail, Bashō is overcome by wanderlust and travels to Nagoya, Ueno, Otsu, and Kyoto. He becomes increasingly ill and dies in Osaka in early autumn.

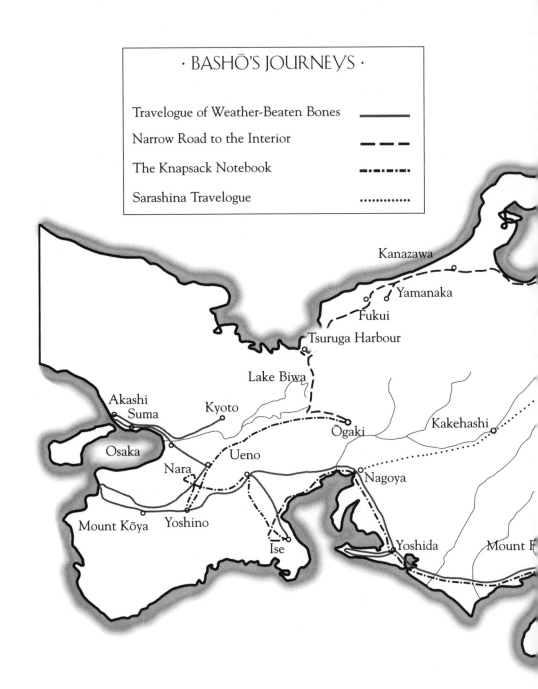

· BASHŌ'S JOURNEYS ·

Travelogue of Weather-Beaten Bones ——————

Narrow Road to the Interior — — —

The Knapsack Notebook —·—·—·—

Sarashina Travelogue ·············

Kisagata

Sakata

Sado Island

Obanazawa

Hiraizumi

Niigata

Matsushima

buri Barrier

Sendai

Iizuka

Ishinomaki

ashina

Nasu Moor

Mount Nikkō

Shirakawa Barrier

Edo

one

Kashima

N

NARROW ROAD
TO THE INTERIOR

THE MOON AND SUN ARE eternal travelers.[1] Even the years wander on. A lifetime adrift in a boat, or in old age leading a tired horse into the years, every day is a journey, and the journey itself is home. From the earliest times there have always been some who perished along the road.[2] Still I have always been drawn by wind-blown clouds into dreams of a lifetime of wandering. Coming home from a year's walking tour of the coast last autumn, I swept the cobwebs from my hut on the banks of the Sumida just in time for New Year, but by the time spring mists began to rise from the fields, I longed to cross the Shirakawa Barrier into the Northern Interior. Drawn by the wanderer-spirit Dōsojin, I couldn't concentrate on things. Mending my cotton pants, sewing a new strap on my bamboo hat, I daydreamed. Rubbing moxa into my legs to strengthen them, I dreamed a bright moon rising over Matsushima. So I placed my house in another's hands and moved to my patron Mr. Sampū's summer house in preparation for my journey. And I left a verse by my door:

Even this grass hut
may be transformed
into a doll's house[3]

⌒

Very early on the twenty-seventh morning of the third moon, under a
predawn haze, transparent moon barely visible,[4] Mount Fuji just a
shadow, I set out under the cherry blossoms of Ueno and Yanaka.
When would I see them again? A few old friends had gathered in the
night and followed along far enough to see me off from the boat. Get-
ting off at Senju, I felt three thousand miles rushing through my heart,
the whole world only a dream. I saw it through farewell tears.

Spring passes
and the birds cry out—tears
in the eyes of fishes

With these first words from my brush, I started. Those who remain
behind watch the shadow of a traveler's back disappear.

⌒

The second year of Genroku, I think of the long way leading into the
Northern Interior under Go stone skies.[5] My hair may turn white as
frost before I return from those fabled places—or maybe I won't return
at all. By nightfall, we come to Soka, bony shoulders sore from heavy
pack, grateful for a warm night robe, cotton bathing gown, writing
brush, ink stone, necessities. The pack made heavier by farewell gifts
from friends. I couldn't leave them behind.

⌒

Continuing on to the shrine at Muro-no-Yashima, my companion Sora said, "This deity, Ko-no-hana Sakuya Hime, is Goddess of Blossoming Trees and also has a shrine at Fuji. She locked herself inside a fire to prove her son's divinity. Thus her son was called Prince Hohodemi—Born-of-Fire—here in Muro-no-Yashima [Burning Cell]. And that's why poets here write of smoke, and why the locals despise the splotched konoshiro[6] fish that reeks like burning flesh. Everyone here knows the story."

The last night of the third moon, an inn at the foot of Mount Nikkō. The innkeeper is called Hotoke Gozaemon, "Joe Buddha." He says his honesty earned him the name and invites me to make myself at home. A merciful buddha suddenly appearing like an ordinary man to help a pilgrim along his way, his simplicity's a great gift, his sincerity unaffected. A model of Confucian rectitude, my host is a bodhisattva.

On the first day of the fourth moon, climbed to visit the shrines on a mountain once called Two Wildernesses, renamed by Kūkai[7] when he dedicated the shrine. Perhaps he saw a thousand years into the future, this shrine under sacred skies, his compassion endlessly scattered through the eight directions, falling equally, peaceably, on all four classes of people. The greater the glory, the less these words can say.

Ah—speechless before
these budding green spring leaves
in blazing sunlight

Mount Kurokami still clothed in snow, faint in the mist, Sora wrote:

> Head shaven
> at Black Hair Mountain
> we change into summer clothes

Sora was named Kawai Sogoro. Sora's his nom de plume. At my old home—called Bashō-an [plantain tree hermitage]—he carried water and wood. Anticipating the pleasures of seeing Matsushima and Kisa-gata, we agreed to share the journey, pleasure and hardship alike. The morning we started, he put on Buddhist robes, shaved his head, and changed his name to Sogo, the Enlightened. So the "changing clothes" in his poem is pregnant with meaning.[8]

A hundred yards uphill, the waterfall plunged a hundred feet from its cavern in the ridge, falling into a basin made by a thousand stones. Crouched in the cavern behind the falls, looking out, I under-stood why it's called Urami-no-Taki [View-from-behind Falls].

> Stopped awhile
> inside a waterfall—
> summer retreat begins[9]

A friend lives in Kurobane on the far side of the broad Nasu Moor. Tried a shortcut running straight through, but it began to rain in the early evening, so we stopped for the night at a village farmhouse and continued again at dawn. Out in the field, a horse, and nearby a man cutting grass. I stopped to ask directions. Courteous, he thought awhile, then said, "Too many intersecting roads. It's easy to get lost. Best to take that old horse as far as he'll go. He knows the road. When he stops, get off, and he'll come back alone."

Two small children danced along behind, one with the curious name of Kasane, same as the pink flower. Sora wrote:

With this *kasane*
she's doubly pink
a fitting name

Arriving at a village, I tied a small gift to the saddle, and the horse turned back.

⌢

Once in Kurobane, I visited the powerful samurai Joboji, overseer of the manor. Surprised by the visit, he kept me up talking through several days and nights, often at the home of his brother Tosui. We visited their relatives and friends. One day we walked out to Inu-oumono, Dog-shooting Grounds. We walked out into the moors to find the tomb of Lady Tamamo, who turned herself to stone. [10] We paid homage at Hachiman Shrine where Yoshitsune's General Yoichi shot a fan from a passing boat after praying to Sho-hachiman, warrior god of this shrine.[11] At dusk we returned to Tosui's home.

Invited to visit Shūgen Kōmyō Temple's hall for mountain monks:

In summer mountains
bow to holy high-water clogs[12]
bless this long journey

Not far from the temple, in a mountain hermitage near Ungan Temple, my dharma master Butchō[13] wrote:

> A five-foot thatched hut—
> I wouldn't even put it up
> but for falling rain

He inscribed the poem on a rock with charcoal—he told me long ago. Curious, several young people joined in, walking sticks pointed toward Ungan Temple. We were so caught up in talking we arrived at the temple unexpectedly. Through the long valley, under dense cedar and pine with dripping moss, below a cold spring sky—through the viewing gardens, we crossed a bridge and entered the temple gate.

I searched out back for Butchō's hermitage and found it up the hill, near a cave on a rocky ridge—like the cave where Myozenji lived for fifteen years, like Zen master Houn's retreat.[14]

> Even woodpeckers
> leave it alone—hermitage
> in a summer grove

One small poem, quickly written, pinned to a post.

Set out to see the Murder Stone, Sessho-seki, on a borrowed horse, and the man leading it asked for a poem, "Something beautiful, please."

The horse turns his head—
from across the wide plain,
a cuckoo's cry

Sessho-seki lies in dark mountain shadow near a hot springs emitting
bad gases. Dead bees and butterflies cover the sand.

⌒

At Ashino, the willow Saigyō[15] praised, "beside the clear stream,"
still grows along a path in fields of rice. A local official had offered to
lead the way, and I had often wondered whether and where it re-
mained. And now, today, that same willow:

Rice-planting done, they
depart—before I emerge
from willow shade[16]

⌒

A little anxious, thinking of the Shirakawa Barrier, thinking on it day
by day; but calmed my mind by remembering the old poem, "somehow
sending word home." I walked through heavy green summer forests.
Many a poet inscribed a few words at one of the Three Barriers—
"Autumn Winds" and "Red Maple Leaves" come to mind.[17] Then,
like fields of snow, innumerable white-flowered bushes, unohana, cov-
ered either side of the road. Here, Kiyosuke[18] wrote, people dressed
their very best to pass through the mountain gate, men in small black
formal hats as though dressed for the highest courts.

Unohana
around my head
dressed for ancient rites   [SORA]

Over the pass, we crossed the Abukuma River, Mount Aizu to the left, the villages of Iwaki, Soma, and Miharu, divided from the villages of Hitachi and Shimotsuke by two small mountain ranges on the right. At Kagenuma, the Mirror Pond, a dark sky blurred every reflection.

We spent several days in Sukagawa with the poet Tōkyu, who asked about the Shirakawa Barrier. "With mind and body sorely tested," I answered, "busy with other poets' lines, engaged in splendid scenery, it's hardly surprising I didn't write much:

Culture's beginnings:
from the heart of the country
rice-planting songs

"From this opening verse," I told him, "we wrote three linked-verse poems."

In the shade of a huge chestnut at the edge of town, a monk made his hermitage a refuge from the world. Saigyō's poem about gathering chestnuts deep in the mountains refers to such a place. I wrote on a slip of paper: The Chinese character for "chestnut" means "west tree," alluding to the Western Paradise of Amida Buddha; the priest Gyōki,[19] all his life, used chestnut for his walking stick and for the posts of his home.

Almost no one sees
the blossoming chestnut
under the eaves

Walked a few miles from Tōkyu's home to the town of Hiwada in the foothills of Mount Asaka. Marshlands glistened outside of town. Almost midsummer, iris-picking time. I asked about blossoming *katsumi*, but no one knew where they grew. I searched all day, muttering "*Katsumi, katsumi*," until the sun set over the mountains.

We followed a road to the right at Nihonmatsu and stopped to see Kurozuka Cave. And stayed the night in Fukushima.

At dawn we left for Shinobu, famous for dyed cloth—called *shinobu-zuri*—named after the rock we found half-buried in the mountain. Village children joined us and explained, "In the old days, the rock was on top of the mountain, but visitors trampled farmers' crops and picked grain, so the old men rolled it down." Their story made perfect sense.

> Girls' busy hands
> plant rice almost like
> the ancient ones made dye

Crossed on the ferry at Tsukinowa to the post town of Se-no-ue to see the ruins that were Satō Shōji's house, beyond town to the left, near the mountains. We were told to look at Saba Moor in Iizuka, and we eventually came to Maru Hill where the castle ruins lay. Seeing the main gate sundered, the ancient temple nearby, seeing all the family graves, my eyes glazed with tears. Especially at the tombs of two young widows who had dressed in the armor of fallen sons and then lay down their lives. Like Tu Yu at Weeping Gravemound, I dried my eyes with a sleeve. Inside the temple, enjoying tea, seeing Yoshitsune's[20] great long sword and the priest Benkei's[21] little Buddhist wicker chest, both enshrined:

Sword, chest, and wind-carp
all proudly displayed
on Boys' Festival Day

It was the first of Satsuki, rice-planting month.

Staying the night in Iizuka, we bathed in a mineral hot springs before returning to thin straw sleeping mats on bare ground—a true country inn. Without a lamp, we made our beds by firelight, in flickering shadows, and closed our tired eyes. Suddenly a thunderous downpour and leaky roof aroused us, fleas and mosquitoes everywhere. Old infirmities tortured me throughout the long, sleepless night.

At first light, long before dawn, we packed our things and left, distracted, tired, but moving on. Sick and worried, we hired horses to ride to the town of Kori. I worried about my plans. With every pilgrimage one encounters the temporality of life. To die along the road is destiny. Or so I told myself. I stiffened my will and, once resolute, crossed Okido Barrier in Date Province.

Through narrow Abumizuri Pass and on, passing Shiroishi Castle, we entered Kasashima Province. We asked for directions to the gravemound of Lord Sanekata, Sei Shonagon's exiled poet-lover, and were told to turn right on the hills near the villages of Minowa and Kasa-

shima when we came to the shrine of Dōsojin. It lies nearly hidden in
sedge grass Saigyō remembered in a poem. May rains turned the trail
to mud. We stopped, sick and worn out, and looked at the two aptly
named villages in the distance: Straw Raincoat Village and Umbrella
Island.

> Where's Kasashima?
> Lost in the rainy season
> on a muddy road

The night was spent in Iwanuma.

―

Deeply touched by the famous pine at Takekuma, twin trunks just as
long ago. The poet-priest Nōin came to mind. Before he came, Lord
Fujiwara-no Takayoshi cut down the tree for lumber, building a
bridge across the Natorigawa. Nōin wrote: "No sign here now of that
famous pine." Reported to have been cut down and replaced several
times, it stood like a relic of a thousand years, impossibly perfect. The
poet Kyōhaku had given me a poem at my departure:

> Remember to show my master
> the famous Takekuma pine,
> O northern blossoming cherries

To which I now reply:

> Ever since cherry blossom time
> I longed to visit the famous split pine:
> three long months have passed

We crossed over the Natorigawa on the seventh day, fifth moon, and entered Sendai on the day we tie blue iris to the eaves and pray for health. We found an inn and decided to spend several days. I'd heard of a painter here, Kaemon, who was a kindred spirit and had visited all the nearby places the poets had made famous. Before him, these places were all but forgotten. He agreed to be our guide. The fields at Miyagi were carpeted with bush clover that would bloom in autumn. In Tamada, Yokono, and at Azalea Hill there were andromeda flowers in bloom. Passing through pine woods sunlight couldn't penetrate, we came to Konoshita, the "Under Woods" where the *Kokinshū* poet begged an umbrella for his lord in falling dew. We visited Yakushido Shrine and the Shrine of Tenjin[22] until the sun went down. Later the painter gave us drawings of Matsushima and Shiogama. And two pairs of new straw sandals with iris-blue straps—*hanamuke*, farewell gifts. He was a truly kindred spirit.

> To have blue irises
> blooming on one's feet—
> walking-sandal straps

Checking Kaemon's drawings as we walked, we followed the *oku-no-hosomichi* along the mountainside where sedge grass grew tall in bunches. The Tofu area is famous for its sedge mats sent in tribute to the governor each year.

At Taga Castle, we found the most ancient monument Tsubo-no-ishibumi, in Ichikawa Village. It's about six feet high and three feet wide. We struggled to read the inscription under heavy moss:

This Castle Was Built by Shogun Ono-no-Azumabito in 724. In 762, His Majesty's Commanding General Emi-no-Asakari Supervised Repairs.

Dated from the time of Emperor Shomu, Tsubo-no-ishibumi inspired many a poet. Floods and landslides buried trails and markers, trees have grown and died, making this monument very difficult to find. The past remains hidden in clouds of memory. Still it returned us to memories from a thousand years before. Such a moment is the reason for a pilgrimage: infirmities forgotten, the ancients remembered, joyous tears trembled in my eyes.

~

We stopped along the Tama River at Noda, and at the huge stone in the lake, Oki-no-ishi, both made famous in poems. On Mount Sue-no-matsu, we found a temple called Masshozan. There were graves everywhere among the pines, underscoring Po Chu-i's famous lines quoted in The Tale of Genji, "wing and wing, branch and branch," and I thought, "Yes, what we all must come to," my sadness heavy.

At Shiogama Beach, a bell sounded evening. The summer rain-sky cleared to reveal a pale moon high over Magaki Island. I remembered the "fishing boats pulling together" in a Kokinshū poem, and understood it clearly for the first time.

Along the Michinoku
everyplace is wonderful,
but in Shiogama
fishing boats pulling together
are most amazing of all.

That night we were entertained by a blind singer playing a lute to boisterous back-country ballads one hears only deep inside the country, not like the *Tale of the Heike* songs or the dance songs. A real earful, but pleased to hear the tradition continued.

⁓

Rose at dawn to pay respects at Myōjin Shrine in Shiogama. The former governor rebuilt it with huge, stately pillars, bright painted rafters, and a long stone walkway rising steeply under a morning sun that danced and flashed along the red lacquered fence. I thought, "As long as the road is, even if it ends in dust, the gods come with us, keeping a watchful eye. This is our culture's greatest gift." Kneeling at the shrine, I noticed a fine old lantern with this inscribed on its iron grate:

In the Third Year of the Bunji Era [1187]
Dedicated by Izumi Saburo

Suddenly, five long centuries passed before my eyes. He was a trusted, loyal man martyred by his brother; today there's not a man alive who doesn't revere his name. As he himself would say, a man must follow the Confucian model—renown will inevitably result.

⁓

Sun high overhead before we left the shrine, we hired a boat to cross to Matsushima, a mile or more away. We disembarked on Ojima Beach.

As many others often observed, the views of Matsushima take one's breath away. It may be—along with Lake Tung-t'ing and West Lake in China—the most beautiful place in the world. Islands in a three-mile bay, the sea to the southeast entering like flood tide on the Ch'ien-t'ang River in Chekiang. Small islands, tall islands pointing at the sky, islands on top of islands, islands like mothers with baby islands on their backs, islands cradling islands in the bay. All covered with deep green pines shaped by salty winds, trained into sea-wind bonsai. Here one is almost overcome by the sense of intense feminine beauty in a shining world. It must have been the mountain god Oya-mazumi who made this place. And whose words or brush could adequately describe a world so divinely inspired?

~

Ojima Beach is not—as its name implies—an island, but a strand projected into the bay. Here one finds the ruins of Ungo Zenji's[23] hermitage and the rock where he sat *zazen*. And still a few tiny thatched huts under pines where religious hermits live in tranquility. Smoke of burning leaves and pine cones drew me on, touching something deep inside. Then the moon rose, shining on the sea, day turned suddenly to night. We stayed at an inn on the shore, our second-story windows opening on the bay. Drifting with winds and clouds, it was almost like a dream. Sora wrote:

> In Matsushima
> you'll need the wings of a crane
> little cuckoo

I was speechless and tried to sleep, but rose to dig from my pack a Chinese-style poem my friend Sodo had written for me, something about Pine Islands. And also a *waka* by Hara Anteki, and haiku by Sampū and Jokushi.

~

On the eleventh day, fifth moon, we visited Zuigan Temple, and were met by the thirty-second-generation descendent of the founder. Established by Makabe-no-Heishiro at the time he returned from religious studies in T'ang China, the temple was enlarged under Ungo Zenji into seven main structures with new blue tile roofs, walls of gold, a jeweled buddha-land. But my mind wandered, wondering if the priest Kembutsu's[24] tiny temple might be found.

—

Early morning of the twelfth day, fifth moon. We started out for Hiraizumi, intending to go by way of the famous Aneha Pine and the Odae Bridge. The trail was narrow and little traveled—only the occasional woodcutter or hunter. We took a wrong road and ended up in the port town of Ishinomaki on a broad bay with Mount Kinka in the distance. Yakamochi has a poem for the emperor in the *Man'yōshū* saying Kinka is "where gold blossoms." It rises across water cluttered with cargo boats and fishing boats, shoreline packed with houses, smoke rising from their stoves. Our unplanned visit prompted an immediate search for lodging. No one made an offer. Spent the night in a cold shack and left again at daybreak, following unknown paths. We passed near the Sode Ferry, Obuchi Meadow, and the Mano Moor—all made famous in poems. After crossing a long miserable marsh, we stayed at Toima, pushing on to Hiraizumi in the morning. An arduous trek of over forty difficult miles in two days.

—

Here three generations of the Fujiwara clan passed as though in a dream. The great outer gates lay in ruins. Where Hidehira's manor stood, rice fields grew. Only Mount Kinkei remained. I climbed the hill where Yoshitsune died; I saw the Kitakami, a broad stream flowing down through the Nambu Plain, the Koromo River circling Izumi Castle below the hill before joining the Kitakami. The ancient ruins of Yasuhira—from the end of the Golden Era—lie out beyond the Koromo Barrier, where they stood guard against the Ainu people. The faithful elite remained bound to the castle—for all their valor, reduced to ordinary grass. Tu Fu wrote:

> The whole country devastated
> only mountains and rivers remain.
> In springtime, at the ruined castle,
> the grass is always green.

We sat a while, our hats for a seat, seeing it all through tears.

> Summer grasses:
> all that remains of great soldiers'
> imperial dreams[25]

⌒

Sora wrote:

> Kanefusa's[26]
> own white hair
> seen in blossoming briar

⌒

Two temple halls I longed to see were finally opened at Chūson Temple. In the Sutra Library, Kyōdō, statues of the three generals of Hiraizumi; and in the Hall of Light, Hikaridō, their coffins and images of three buddhas. It would have all fallen down, jeweled doors battered by winds, gold pillars cracked by cold, all would have gone to grass, but added outer roof and walls protect it. Through the endless winds and rains of a thousand years, this great hall remains.

Fifth-month rains hammer
and blow but never quite touch
Hikaridō

The road through the Nambu Plain visible in the distance, we stayed the night in Iwate, then trudged on past Cape Oguro and Mizu Island, both along the river. Beyond Narugo Hot Springs, we crossed Shito-mae Barrier and entered Dewa Province. Almost no one comes this way, and the barrier guards were suspicious, slow, and thorough. Delayed, we climbed a steep mountain in falling dark, and took refuge in a guardshack. A heavy storm pounded the shack with wind and rain for three miserable days.

Eaten alive by
lice and fleas—now the horse
beside my pillow pees

The guard told us, "To get to Dewa, you'd better take a guide. There's a high mountain and a hard-to-find trail." He found us a powerful young man, short sword on his hip and oak walking stick in hand, and off we went, not without a little trepidation. As forewarned, the mountain was steep, the trail narrow, not even a birdcall to be heard. We made our way through deep forest dark as night, reminding me of Tu Fu's poem about "clouds bringing darkness." We groped through thick bamboo, waded streams, climbed through rocks, sweaty, fearful, and tired, until we finally came to the village of Mogami. Our guide, turning back, said again how the trail was tough. "Happy you didn't meet many surprises!" And departed. Hearing this, our hearts skipped another beat.

—

Visited a merchant in Obanazawa, a Mr. Seifu, finding him to be wealthy but relatively free of the vulgarities of the merchant class. And he knew from his own many travels to Miyako the trials of life on the road, so invited us to stay the week. All in all, quite relaxing.

"My house is your house,"
and so it is—very cool,
sprawling out in comfort

Come out from hiding
under the silkworm room
little demon toad voice!

A little rouge brush,
reminding me somehow
of local safflower fields

Sora wrote:

Women in the silkworm room
all dressed simply—like women
in antiquity

—

In Yamagata Province, the ancient temple founded by Jikaku Daishi in 860, Ryūshaku Temple is stone quiet, perfectly tidy. Everyone told us to see it. It meant a few miles extra, doubling back toward Obanazawa to find shelter. Monks at the foot of the mountain offered rooms, then we climbed the ridge to the temple, scrambling up through ancient gnarled pine and oak, gray smooth stones and moss. The temple doors, built on rocks, were bolted. I crawled among boulders to make my bows at shrines. The silence was profound. I sat, feeling my heart begin to open.

> Lonely stillness—
> a single cicada's cry
> sinking into stone

Planning to ride down the Mogami River, we were delayed at Oishida, waiting for decent weather. "This is haiku country," someone told us, "seeds from old days blooming like forgotten flowers, the sound of a bamboo flute moving the heart. With no one to show us the way, however, local poets try new style and old style together." So we made a small anthology together, but the result is of little merit. So much for culture.

The Mogami flows from the Michinoku at the far northern edge of Yamagata country. It is dangerous through Go Stone Rapids and Falcon Rapids, circumscribing northern Mount Itajiki to meet the sea at Sakata. Mountains rose from either side of the boat as we sped between the trees. The boat was only a tiny rice-boat not meant for all we carried. We passed Shiraito Falls where it tumbles under pines. Hall of Immortals on the riverbank.[27] The waters so high, it was a dangerous ride.

All the summer rains
violently gather—
Mogami River

—

Climbed Mount Haguro on the third day of the sixth moon and, with
the help of a friend who dyes cloth for mountain monks' robes, Zushi
Sakichi, obtained an audience with the abbot of Gongen Shrine, Mas-
ter Egaku, who greeted us warmly. He arranged for quarters at nearby
South Valley Temple. The next day we met at the main temple to
write haiku:

The winds that blow
through South Valley Temple
are sweetened by snow[28]

—

We paid homage at Gongen Shrine on the fifth. The first shrine on
the mountain, it was built by Nojo, no one knows exactly when. The
Engi Ceremonies calls it Ushusato Mountain, Feather Province Village
Mountain, but calligraphers' errors got it changed to Feather *Black*
Mountain. The province is called Dewa, Feather Tribute, dating from
an eighth-century custom whereby feather down from this region was
used as payment of tribute. Together with Moon Mountain and Bath
Mountain, Feather Black Mountain completes the Dewa Sanzan, or
Three Holy Mountains of Dewa. This temple is Tendai sect, like the
one in Edo on Toei Hill. Both follow the doctrine of *shikantaza*, "deep-
sitting concentration and insight," a way of enlightenment as transpar-
ent as moonlight, its light infinitely increasing, spreading from hermit-
age to mountaintop and back, reverence and compassion shining in

everything it touches. Its blessing flows down from these mountains, enriching all our lives.

———

On the eighth we climbed Moon Mountain, wearing the holy paper necklaces and cotton hats of Shinto priests, following behind a mountain monk whose footsteps passed through mist and clouds and snow and ice, climbing miles higher as though drawn by invisible spirits into the gateway of the sky—sun, moon, and clouds floated by and took my breath away. Long after sunset, moon high over the peak, we reached the summit, spread out in bamboo grass, and slept. Next day, after the sun burned away the clouds, we started down toward Yudono, Bath Mountain.

Approaching the valley, we passed Swordsmith Hut, named for the twelfth-century smith, Gassan, who purified himself with holy water here and used it to temper his blades. On each blade he inscribed "Gassan," Moon Mountain. He admired the famous Dragon Spring swords of China. I remembered the legendary man-and-wife smiths renowned for their dedication to detail and technique.

We stretched on a rock to rest and noticed the opening buds of a three-foot cherry tree. Buried under stubborn snow, it insists on honoring spring however late it arrives. Like the Chinese poem, "Plum blossoms fragrant in burning sun!" And Gyōson Sōjō[29] wrote, "So sad, blossoming cherry, you have no one to admire you." It's all here, in these tiny blossoms!

To say more is sacrilege. Forbidden to speak, put down the brush, respect Shinto rites. Later, back with Master Egaku, we wrote poems on the Three Holy Mountains:

Cool crescent moon
shining faintly high above
Feather Black Mountain

How many rising
clouds collapse and fall on
this moonlit mountain

Forbidden to speak
alone on Yudono Mountain
tears soak through my sleeves

Sora wrote:

Bath Mountain walkway
paved with pilgrims' coins:
here too are tears

After leaving Haguro, we came to the castle town of Tsuru-ga-oka
accompanied by Zushi Sakichi, and were greeted by the samurai Na-
gayama Shigeyuki. We composed a round of haiku, bid farewell, and
started by boat down the Mogami, bound for Sakata Harbor. We
stayed overnight with a certain doctor who wrote under the nom de
plume En-an Fugyoku.

From Hot Sea Mountain
southward to Windy Beach
the evening cools

A burning summer sun
slowly going down to drown—
Mogami River

⁓

After all the breathtaking views of rivers and mountains, lands and
seas, after everything we'd seen, thoughts of seeing Kisakata's famous
bay still made my heart begin to race. Twenty miles north of Sakata
Harbor, as we walked the sandy shore beneath mountains where sea
winds wander, a storm came up at dusk and covered Mount Chokai
in mist and rain reminiscent of Su Tung-p'o's famous poem. We made
our way in the dark, hoping for a break in the weather, groping on
until we found a fisherman's shack. By dawn the sky had cleared, sun
dancing on the harbor. We took a boat for Kisakata, stopping by the
priest Nōin's island retreat, honoring his three-year seclusion. On the
opposite shore we saw the ancient cherry tree Saigyō saw reflected
and immortalized, "Fishermen row over blossoms."

Near the shore, Empress Jingū's tomb. And Kammanju Temple.
Did the empress ever visit? Why is she buried here?

Sitting in the temple chamber with the blinds raised, we saw
the whole lagoon, Mount Chōkai holding up the heavens inverted on
the water.[30] To the west the road leads to the Muyamuya Barrier; to
the east it curves along a bank toward Akita; to the north, the sea
comes in on tide flats at Shiogoshi. The whole lagoon, though only a
mile or so across, reminds one of Matsushima, although Matsushima
seems much more contented, whereas Kisakata seems bereaved. A sad-
ness maybe in its sense of isolation here where nature's darker spirits
hide—like a strange and beautiful woman whose heart has been
broken.

Kisakata rain:
the legendary beauty Seishi
wrapped in sleeping leaves

At the Shallows
the long-legged crane cool,
stepping in the sea

Sora wrote:

Kisakata Festival—
at holy feasts, what specialties
do the locals eat?

The merchant Teiji from Minō Province wrote:

Fishermen sit
on their shutters on the sand
enjoying cool evening

Sora found an osprey nest in the rocks:

May the ocean resist
violating the vows
of the osprey's nest

After several days, clouds gathering over the North Road, we left Sakata reluctantly, aching at the thought of a hundred thirty miles to the provincial capital of Kaga. We crossed the Nezu Barrier into

Echigo Province, and from there went on to Ichiburi Barrier in Etchu, restating our resolve all along the way. Through nine hellish days of heat and rain, all my old maladies tormenting me again, feverish and weak, I could not write.

> Altair meets Vega
> tomorrow—Tanabata—
> already the night is changed[31]

> High over wild seas
> surrounding Sado Island—
> the River of Heaven[32]

Today we came through places with names like Children-Desert-Parents, Lost Children, Send-Back-the-Dog, Turn-Back-the-Horse, some of the most fearsomely dangerous places in all the North Country. And well named. Weakened and exhausted, I went to bed early, but was roused by the voices of two young women in the room next door. Then an old man's voice joined theirs. They were prostitutes from Niigata in Echigo Province and were on their way to Ise Shrine in the south, the old man seeing them off at this barrier, Ichiburi. He would turn back to Niigata in the morning, carrying their letters home. One girl quoted the *Shinkokinshū* poem, "On the beach where white waves fall, / we all wander like children into every circumstance, / carried forward every day . . ." And as they bemoaned their fate in life, I fell asleep.

In the morning, preparing to leave, they came to ask directions. "May we follow along behind?" they asked. "We're lost and not a little fearful. Your robes bring the spirit of the Buddha to our journey." They had mistaken us for priests. "Our way includes detours and retreats," I told them. "But follow anyone on this road and the gods will see you through." I hated to leave them in tears, and thought about them hard for a long time after we left. I told Sora, and he wrote down:

> Under one roof,
> courtesans and monks asleep—
> moon and bush clover

⁓

We managed to cross all "forty-eight rapids" of the Kurobe River on our way to the bay of Nago. Although it was no longer spring, we thought even an autumn visit to the wisteria at Tako—made famous in the *Man'yōshū*—worth the trouble, and asked the way: "Five miles down the coast, then up and over a mountain. A few fishermen's shacks, but no lodging, no place even to camp." It sounded so difficult, we pushed on instead into the province of Kaga.

> Fragrance of rice
> as we pass by—to the right,
> Ariso Sea

⁓

We crossed Mount Unohana and Kurikara Valley at noon on the fifteenth day of the seventh moon and entered Kanazawa, where we took rooms at an inn with a merchant from Osaka, a Mr. Kasho, who was in town to attend memorial services for the haiku poet Isshō, locally renowned for his verse and devotion to craft. The poet's elder brother served as host, the poet having died last winter.

Tremble, oh my grave—
in time my cries will be
only this autumn wind

~

We were invited to visit a thatched-roof hermitage:

Autumn's very cool—
our hands busy peeling
melon and eggplant

Later, written along the road:

Intense hot red sun,
heartlessly—but already
autumn in the wind

~

At a village called Komatsu:

Aptly named Komatsu,
Child Pine, a breeze blows over
pampas and clover

Here we visited Tada Shrine to see Sanemori's[33] helmet and a piece of
his brocade armor-cloth presented to him by Lord Yoshitomo when
he served the Genji clan. His helmet was no common soldier's gear:
engraved with chrysanthemums and ivy from eyehole to earflap,
crowned with a dragon's head between two horns. After Sanemori
died on the battlefield, Kiso Yoshinaka sent it with a prayer, hand-

carried to the shrine by Higuchi Jirō, Sanemori's friend. The story's inscribed on the shrine.

> Pitifully—under
> a great soldier's empty helmet,
> a cricket sings

—

Along the road to Yamanaka Hot Springs, Mount Shirane rose behind our backs. At the foot of a mountain to our left we found a small temple to compassionate Kannon. After the retired Emperor Kazan had made a pilgrimage to the thirty-three western temples, he enshrined an image of the bodhisattva Kannon here, naming the temple Nata, using the first syllables of the first and last temples of the thirty-three: Nachi and Tanigumi. A small thatched-roof temple built on a rock among boulders and twisted pines, Nata lingers in the mind:

> Whiter than the stones
> of Stone Mountain Temple—
> autumn wind blows

—

We bathed in mineral hot springs comparable to those at Ariake.

> After hours bathing
> in Yamanaka's waters—
> couldn't even pick a flower

Our host at the inn was a young man named Kumenosuke. His father was a knowledgeable haiku poet who had embarrassed the poet Teishitsu of Kyoto when Teishitsu was still ignorant and young. The latter thus returned to Kyoto and apprenticed himself to haiku master Teitoku.[34] When Teishitsu returned to Yamanaka to judge a poetry contest, he refused to accept payment, having been so humbled. It's a legend around here now.

―

Sora, suffering from persistent stomach ailments, was forced to return to his relatives in Nagashima in Ise Province. His parting words:

> Sick to the bone
> if I should fall, I'll lie
> in fields of clover

He carries his pain as he goes, leaving me empty. Like paired geese parting in the clouds.[35]

> Now falling autumn dew
> obliterates my hatband's
> "We are two"[36]

―

I stayed at Zenshō-ji, a temple near the castle town of Daishōji in Kaga Province. It was from this temple that Sora departed last night, leaving behind:

> All night long
> listening to autumn winds
> wandering in the mountains

One night like a thousand miles, as the proverb says, and I too listened to fall winds howl around the same temple. But at dawn, the chanting of sutras, gongs ringing, awakened me. An urgent need to leave for distant Echizen Province. As I prepared to leave the temple, two young monks arrived with ink stone and paper in hand. Outside, willow leaves fell in the wind.

> Sweep the garden—
> all kindnesses falling
> willow leaves repay

My sandals already on, I wrote it quickly and departed.

At the Echizen Province border, at an inlet town called Yoshizaki, I hired a boat and sailed for the famous pines of Shiogoshi. Saigyō wrote:

> All the long night
> salt-winds drive
> storm-tossed waves
> and moonlight drips
> through Shiogoshi pines.

This one poem says enough. To add another would be like adding a sixth finger to a hand.[37]

In the town of Matsuoka, I visited Tenryū Temple, renewing an old friendship with the elder. The poet Hokushi from Kanazawa, intending only to see me off a way, had come this far with me, but turned back here. His poems on views along the way were sensitive, and I wrote for him:

Writing on my fan,
now it's torn in half—
for memory's sake

⁓

Walked a few miles into the mountains to pray at Dōgen Zenji's[38] temple, Eihei-ji. To have placed it here, "a thousand miles from the capital," as the old saying goes, was no accident.

⁓

After supper, I set out for Fukui, five miles down the road, the way made difficult by falling dark. An old recluse named Tōsai lived somewhere around here. More than ten years had passed since he came to visit me in Edo. Was he still alive? I was told he still lived near town, a small, weathered house just off the road, lost in tangles of gourd-vines growing under cypress. I found the gate and knocked. A lonely-looking woman answered. "Where do you come from, honorable priest? The master has gone to visit friends." Probably his wife, she looked like she'd stepped right out of *Genji*.

I found Tōsai and stayed two days before deciding to leave to see the full moon at Tsuruga Harbor. Tōsai, enthused, tied up his robes in his sash, and we set off with him serving as guide.

⁓

Mount Shirane faded behind us and Mount Hina began to appear. We crossed Asamuzu Bridge and saw the legendary "reeds of Tamae" in bloom. We crossed Uguisu Barrier at Yuno-o Pass and passed by the ruins of Hiuchi Castle. On Returning Hill we heard the first wild geese of autumn. We arrived at Tsuruga Harbor on the evening of the fouteenth day of the eighth moon. The harbor moonlight was marvelously bright.

I asked at the inn, "Will we have this view tomorrow night?" The innkeeper said, "Can't guarantee weather in Koshiji. It may be clear, but then again it may turn overcast. It may rain." We drank sake with the innkeeper, then paid a late visit to the Kei Myōjin Shrine honoring the second-century Emperor Chūai. A great spirituality—moonlight in pines, white sands like a touch of frost. In ancient times Yugyō, the second high priest, himself cleared away the grounds, carried stones, and built drains. To this day, people carry sands to the shrine. "Yugyō-no-sunamochi," the innkeeper explained, "Yugyō's sand-bringing."

Transparent moonlight,
just as it shone when Yugyō
carried sand to the shrine

⌒

On the fifteenth, just as the innkeeper predicted, it rained:

A harvest moon, but
true North Country weather—
nothing to view

⌒

The sky cleared the morning of the sixteenth. I sailed to Iro Beach a dozen miles away and gathered several colorful shells with a Mr.

Tenya, who provided a box lunch and sake and even invited his servants. Tail winds got us there in a hurry. A few fishermen's shacks dotted the beach, and the tiny Hokke temple was disheveled. We drank tea and hot sake, lost in a sweeping sense of isolation as dusk came on.

> Loneliness greater
> than *Genji's* Suma Beach:
> the shores of autumn

> Wave after wave
> mixes tiny seashells with
> bush clover flowers

Tōsai wrote a record of our afternoon and left it at the temple.

———

A disciple, Rotsū had come to Tsuruga to travel with me to Mino Province. We rode horses into the castle town of Ōgaki. Sora returned from Ise, joined by Etsujin, also riding a horse. We gathered at the home of Jokō, a retired samurai. Lord Zensen, the Keikou men, and other friends arrived by day and night, all to welcome me as though I'd come back from the dead. A wealth of affection!

Still exhausted and weakened from my long journey, on the sixth day of the darkest month, I felt moved to visit Ise Shrine,[39] where a twenty-one-year Rededication Ceremony was about to get underway. At the beach, in the boat, I wrote:

> Clam ripped from its shell,
> I move on to Futami Bay:
> passing autumn

TRAVELOGUE OF
WEATHER-BEATEN BONES

I LEFT MY RUNDOWN HUT beside the river during the eighth month of 1684, placing my trust in my walking stick and in the words of the Chinese sage who said, "I pack no provisions for my long journey—entering emptiness under the midnight moon."[40] The voice of the wind was oddly cold.

Weather-beaten bones,
I'll leave your heart exposed
to cold, piercing winds

After ten autumns,
it is strange to say Edo
speaking of my home

I crossed Hakone Barrier in the rain, clouds hiding all the mountains.

> Heavy falling mist—
> Mount Fuji not visible,
> but still intriguing

My traveling companion, Chiri, inspires confidence and provides every possible comfort. A longtime confidant, he meets the Confucian ideal of "one who is sincere in conversation with friends."

> From Fukagawa
> we depart, leaving Bashō's hut
> in Fuji's custody   [CHIRI]

On the bank of the Fuji River, we came upon an abandoned child, about age two, its sobs stirring our pity. The child's parents must have been crushed by the waves of this floating world to have left him here beside the rushing river to pass like dew. I thought the harsh autumn winds would surely scatter the bush clover blossoms in the night or wither them—and him—in the frosty dew of dawn. I left him what food I could.

> Hearing the monkey's cries—
> what of the child abandoned
> to the autumn wind?

How can this happen? Did his father despise him? Did his mother neglect him? I think not. This must be the will of heaven. We mourn his fate.

Heavy rains delayed our crossing of the flooded Ōi River:

> Autumn rain falls all day—
> many busy hands in Edo—
> Ōi River!   [Chiri]

Waiting, I watched:

> Along the roadside,
> blossoming wild roses
> in my horse's mouth

I rode in thick darkness under the hills, my quirt hanging at my side, the moon almost gone. We traveled many miles without a single cock crow, until, at Sayo-no-nakayama, I was startled awake. I had been dreaming of Tu Mu's[41] great poem, "Departing in Early Morning."

> Nodding off on horseback,
> I dream of distant moons and
> threads of tea-fire smoke

I traveled on to visit an old friend in Ise and stayed about ten days. Early one evening I visited the Outer Shrine of the seat of Shinto religion. Long shadows fell over the First Torii, and a few lamps were already lit. A cold autumn wind came through the sacred mountain pines, piercing to the bone.

The month's last night, moonless—
a thousand-year-old cedar
embraced by the storm

*

I wear no sword at my belt. Rather, I carry a small bag at my shoulder and Buddhist prayer beads in my hands. I may resemble a priest, but am a layman. Although I am a layman, my head is shaved. Although I am not a monk, one with a clean pate is always treated here as a devout Buddhist, and thus excluded from visiting the Inner Shrine.

*

Coming upon a stream at the bottom of the Saigyō Valley, I watched a woman washing potatoes:

She washes potatoes—
if I could be Saigyō,
I'd write her a song

Later that day I stopped by a teahouse where a young woman named Butterfly asked me to write a haiku about her name on a small piece of silk. I wrote:

The orchid's perfume
clings to the butterfly's wings
like temple incense

While visiting a recluse at his hermitage, I wrote:

The ivy's planted—
four or five bamboo stalks
rattle in the storm

I arrived at my old village early in the ninth month. All the grass beside North Hall had been consumed by frost. Nothing was the same. My brothers had grown gray at the temples, wrinkled around their eyes. All we could say was, "How good to be alive to meet again!"

My older brother opened a small amulet, saying, "Bow to your mother's white hair. This is like the famous jeweled box of Urashima Tarō[42]—your own eyebrows have already turned gray!"

I wrote this after we had all shed our tears:

If I took it in hand,
it would melt in my hot tears—
heavy autumn frost

On foot, we crossed Yamato Province to a place called Take-no-uchi in the Katsuge area. This was Chiri's home, so we paused a few days to refresh ourselves. Deep in a bamboo grove, there was a little house:

A cotton-beating bow—
as comforting as a lute
in the bamboo grove

Visiting Taima Temple on Mount Futagami, there was a courtyard pine, "big enough to hide oxen,"[43] that was probably a thousand years old. It no doubt had been spared the ax, despite not being a "sentient being," through its connection to the buddhas. How fortunate!

Monks and morning glories—
through many generations—
the law of the pine

⌒

I wandered on alone into the mountainous heart of the Yoshino region,
where great white clouds piled high among mountain tops and rain
veiled the valleys. A few woodcutters' cabins dotted the hills. The
sound of axes ringing on the western slope were echoed by eastern
mountains, only to be answered by temple bells that reached my very
core.

Of all the men who have entered these mountains to live the
reclusive life, most found solace in ancient poetry, so it might be ap-
propriate to compare this countryside to Mount Lu, where so many
famous Chinese poets sought seclusion.

I found a night's lodging at a temple hostel:

At her fulling block
she makes beautiful music,
the good temple wife

Saigyō's thatched-roof hut once stood a few hundred yards from the
inner temple, and could be reached only by way of a narrow woods-
man's trail. It looked across a deep, breathtaking valley. The "trickling
clear water" made famous by the poet could still be heard.

With clear melting dew,
I'd try to wash away the dust
of this floating world

If Po-i had been Japanese, he'd no doubt have washed his mouth here. If Hsu Yu knew of it, he'd have washed out his ears here.[44]

Autumn sunset had begun while I was still on the mountain trail, so I decided to forego other famous sites, choosing to visit the tomb of Emperor Go Daigo [1288–1339]:

> At the royal tomb—
> and what does it remember,
> this "remembrance grass"?

I followed the Ōmi Road from Yamato through Yamashiro into the Mino area. Beyond the villages of Imasu and Yamanaka was the grave-site of Lady Tokiwa.[45] The poet Moritake [1473–1549], who was also a Shinto priest at Ise, wrote of "autumn wind like Lord Yoshitomo," an apt comparison. I wrote:

> Lord Yoshitomo's
> heart must closely resemble
> this cold autumn wind

At Fuwa Barrier:

> A strong autumn wind—
> farmyards and bamboo thickets
> at Fuwa Pass

I spent a night in Ōgaki, the guest of the haiku poet Bokuin. When I left my home in Musashino, I was prepared to make this long journey even if it meant ending as bones exposed in some field. So:

> Somehow not yet dead
> at the end of my journey—
> this autumn's evening

At Hontō Temple in Kuwana:

> Winter peonies—
> we'll call these plovers in snow
> our winter cuckoos

Tired of my grass pillow, I went out to the beach in the dark before dawn:

> At breaking sunrise,
> glistening whitefish—an inch
> of utter whiteness

I visited Atsuta Shrine only to find it in ruins, collapsing walls overgrown with weeds, ropes marking the sites of former subsidiary shrines, and here and there stones bearing the names of gods no longer worshipped. And yet despite being overgrown with brush and remembrance grass, the grounds were more memorable than they would have been if kept in a state of perfection.

"Remembrance fern"
withers—I bought fresh rice cakes
at the old hotel

Along Nagoya Road, I recited poetry. A poem in jest:

This harsh winter wind
reminds me of Chikusai[46]—
I too brave its blast!

Grass for a pillow,
and a dog also crying,
howling all night

I took a walk to enjoy the snow:

To these good townsfolk
I'd be persuaded to sell
this hat of snow

Watching a traveler:

Even that old horse
is something to see this
snow-covered morning

From a day's walk on the beach:

> Across a dark sea,
> the distant cries of wild ducks
> and faintly, traces of white

As the year came to its end, I continued on my way, removing sandals
here, resting an old walking stick there.

> As the year concludes—
> wanderer's hat on my head,
> sandals on my feet

Writing such poems, I reached my mountain hut in time for New
Year:

> Whose son-in-law brings
> holiday ferns and rice cakes—
> the Year of the Ox

Along the road to Nara:

> Now spring has arrived
> on a mountain with no name
> in early morning haze

I visited Nigatsudō Hall at Tōdai Temple in Nara for the Water
Drawing Ceremony:[47]

Drawing purifying
water—like the monks' footsteps,
so clear and so cool

~

In the capital, I visited a renowned patron of poets, Mitsui Shūfū, in
his mountain estate, and in a plum grove wrote:

White apricot blossoms—
but sometime yesterday
the crane was stolen![48]

The oak's nobility—
indifferent to flowers—
or so it appears

~

On meeting the head priest Ninkō at Saiganji, a temple in Fushimi:

Please anoint my robe
with Fushimi's peach blossom
dew, drop by drop

Crossing a mountain along Ōtsu Road:

Traveling this high
mountain trail, delighted
by wild violets

A view of Lake Biwa:

> Karasaki's pine,
> compared to blossoming cherry,
> looks a bit hazy

⌒

Resting at an inn after lunch:

> Azaleas placed
> carefully—and a woman
> shredding dried codfish

Along my way:

> In fields of blossoming
> rapeseed, they come flower-viewing—
> a flock of sparrows

After twenty years, I met an old friend at Minakuchi:

> While we've lived our lives
> they've survived to still blossom,
> these old cherry trees

⌒

A monk on pilgrimage from Hiru-ga-kojima in Izu Province since last fall heard about me and followed my route to Owari in hopes of becoming my fellow traveler.

Now we're newfound friends,
we'll eat in the barley fields
and share a grass pillow

When he told me that Daiten, abbot at Engakuji, had died during the
first month, I was stunned. I dashed off word to my friend and fellow
poet Kikaku:

Nostalgic for plum,
I bow among white flowers
and the tears begin

I presented this to my friend Tokoku in Nagoya:

On the white poppy,
a butterfly's torn wing
is a keepsake

I stayed once more with Tōyō, leaving this as I turned east again:

The bee emerging
from deep within the peony
departs reluctantly

On a mountain in Kai Province:

A traveler's horse
in a shelter's barley patch
finds solace at last

I returned to my hermitage to recuperate at the end of the fourth
month.

> Time for summer robes—
> I've not yet picked out the lice
> that cling to them!

THE KNAPSACK
NOTEBOOK

WITHIN THIS TEMPORAL BODY composed of a hundred bones and nine holes there resides a spirit which, for lack of an adequate name, I think of as windblown. Like delicate drapery, it may be torn away and blown off by the least breeze. It brought me to writing poetry many years ago, initially for its own gratification, but eventually as a way of life. True, frustration and rejection were almost enough to bring this spirit to silence, and sometimes pride brought it to the brink of vanity. From the writing of the very first line, it has found no contentment as it was torn by one doubt after another. This windblown spirit considered the security of court life at one point; at another, it considered risking a display of its ignorance by becoming a scholar. But its passion for poetry would not permit either. Since it knows no other way than the way of poetry, it has clung to it tenaciously.

Saigyō in poetry, Sōgi in linked verse, Sesshū in painting, Rikyū in the tea ceremony—the spirit that moves them is one spirit. Achiev-

ing artistic excellence, each holds one attribute in common: each re-
mains attuned to nature throughout the four seasons. Whatever is seen
by such a heart and mind is a flower, whatever is dreamed is a moon.
Only a barbarian mind could fail to see the flower; only an animal
mind could fail to dream a moon. The first task for each artist is to
overcome the barbarian or animal heart and mind, to become one with
nature.

⁓

It was mid-autumn under threatening skies when I made up my mind
to begin a journey. Windblown leaves reminded me of all the uncer-
tainties a wanderer faces.

> A wanderer,
> let that be my name—
> the first winter rain

> Every night, you'll sleep deeply
> among camellias

The second verse is a hopeful note written by a poet from Iwaki,
Chōtarō, at Kikaku's house, where they held a farewell party in my
honor.

⁓

> Winter approaches—
> but in spring, you'll see Yoshino
> cherry blossoms

This poem was a gracious gift from Lord Rosen of Taira, and was followed by more such gifts from friends and students, including poems and "sandal-buying money," and other things greatly simplifying my preparations, which often take months. Paper raincoat, hat, stockings to keep me warm through the winter—all were gifts.

There were boating parties, parties at the houses of various friends, and even one at my hermitage. Reveling in ceremonious feasting, one might easily have been seduced by the illusion that some VIP was about to depart.

⌢

From the earliest times, the art of the travel journal has been appreciated by readers. The great Ki-no-Tsurayuki wrote the famous *Tosa Journal*, and Kamo-no-Chomei recorded life in a ten-foot-square hut. The nun Abutsu perfected the genre. All the rest merely imitate these masters. My brush, lacking both wisdom and inspiration, strives vainly to be their equal.

How easy it is to observe that a morning began with rain only to become sunny in the afternoon; that a pine tree stood at a particular place, or to note the name of a river bend. This is what people write in their journals. Nothing's worth noting that is not seen with fresh eyes. You will find in my notebook random observations from along the road, experiences and images that linger in heart and mind—a secluded house in the mountains, a lonely inn on a moor.

I write in my notebook with the intention of stimulating good conversation, hoping that it will also be of use to some fellow traveler. But perhaps my notes are mere drunken chatter, the incoherent babbling of a dreamer. If so, read them as such.

I spent a night at Narumi—

> At Starlit Point,
> peering into the darkness—
> the cries of plovers

The innkeeper showed me a poem written in the hand of Asukai Masaaki, the twelfth-century poet, who wrote it while staying here on his way from Kyoto:

> The old capital
> seems ever more distant
> now that I've paused at
> Narumi Bay to look back
> across this expansive sea.

Then I wrote:

> Barely halfway
> to the capital—already
> clouds promise snow

I decided to visit my merchant-poet friend Tokoku at his hermitage in Hobi, in Mikawa province. I asked another friend, Etsujin, to join me and we walked many miles before coming to Yoshida and finding an inn.

On the coldest night,
we two sleeping together—
how comfortable!

At Amatsu Nawate, I followed a narrow trail through the middle of
rice fields in the teeth of a storm raging in from the sea.

Crossing long fields,
frozen in its saddle,
my shadow creeps by

Point Irago is just a short walk from Hobi Village. But from Ise Prov-
ince, one had to cross an expanse of sea made famous by a poem in the
Man'yōshū. I pocketed a few white Irago stones popular with players
of the board game Go.

Behind me, a southern promontory, Hone Mountain, famous for
attracting the first hawks of the year. As I was trying to remember
several famous poems about hawks:

A hawk! How lucky
to see it flying over
Point Irago

Workers were completing repairs at Atsuta Jingū Shrine:

Polished and polished
until it is clear, the mirror
reflects snow flowers

I was invited to enjoy a brief respite with friends in Nagoya, a short distance to the west:

> Some poor wanderer
> must be crossing snowy Hakone
> Pass this morning

Attending a party with VIPs:

> Pressing out wrinkles
> in my paper robe—proceed
> to the snow-viewing!

> It's good now and then
> to go out snow-viewing
> until I tumble

I was guest of honor at a gathering at a friend's house:

> The scent of early
> plum—searching, I found it
> in the wine cellar

During my visits in Nagoya, I also wrote a number of linked verses with friends from Ōgaki and Gifu. But after several days, I felt the need to press on toward my native country as the year came to its end.

Along my journey
through this temporal world, people
new-year-house-cleaning

They say the ancient poet Sōgi nearly starved to death in the high village of Hinaga. I hired a horse to help me over Walking-stick Pass. Unfamiliar with horses and tack, both saddle and rider took a tumble.

If I'd walked Walking-
stick Pass, I'd not have fallen
from my horse

I wrote the poem above spontaneously. Perhaps influenced by the inevitable melancholy that comes with late autumn, I note the absence of a seasonal word.

Moved to tears by
finding my umbilical cord—
the year concludes[49]

Reluctant to see the year end, I drank until well past midnight on New Year's Eve, only to sleep through the morning on New Year Day:

On the second day,
I'll rise early to welcome
the oncoming spring

Signs of early spring:

This early spring
barely nine days old and all
those fields and mountains!

Withered winter grass—
waves of warm spring air
shimmering just above

I visited the site of a temple built by the great Shunjō in Iga Province in the twelfth century. It was then called Five Mountains New Great Buddha Temple. Only its long name remains to remind one of its illustrious past. The main hall was razed to the foundation. Former priests' quarters are now soaking fields of rice. Green moss covered the tall buddha, leaving only his sublime face exposed. A statue of the founder stood alone among broken pedestals and ruins overgrown with weeds. Even the great temple trees had died.

Reaching almost to
the broken statue's height,
heat waves rise from stone

A world of memory
returns to me when I see
blossoming cherries

⌢

I visited Yamada in Ise:

From what tree's
blossoming, I do not know,
but oh, its sweet scent!

It's a bit too chilly
to be standing naked in
this cold spring storm

⌢

At Bōdai Mountain:

The mountain's sorrows
the sweet potato digger
can readily tell[50]

⌢

Upon meeting my friend Ryū Shōsha, scholar and priest of Ise Shrine:

First, what is the name
of this peculiar grass?—
and gave him a leaf

⌢

I met the son of Ajiro Minbu, another Ise priest. The young man goes by the haiku name Setsudō:

> From an old plum tree
> a mistletoe is blooming—
> blossoming plum

When I wondered aloud why there were no plum trees in the Ise Shrine compound, the old priest said only that one had been planted behind the sacred virgins' quarters.

> How perfectly right—
> behind the shrine-maidens' house,
> a blossoming plum

⌣

> Behind Ise Shrine,
> unseen, hidden by the fence,
> Buddha enters Nirvana

⌣

By the middle of the second month, I longed to depart for Yoshino, where cherries already blossomed in my memory. A friend, Tokoku, promised to join me in my journey, and we met at Ise. He too antici-pated the many beautiful views we would enjoy while he helped me on my way. He adopted the pen name Mangiku-maru, which I liked. We ceremoniously wrote on our hats, "No home in the world—we are two wanderers," and set out.

> It won't be long till
> you'll see Yoshino cherries,
> my bark-woven hat!

Mangiku-maru wrote:

> It won't be long till
> I show my bark-woven hat
> to Yoshino cherries!

⁓

I believe in traveling light. I sought things I might dispose of, but most were necessities. I had to carry raincoat and overcoat, ink stone, brush, writing paper, various medicines, lunch box—a load. With each slow step, my knees ached and I grew increasingly depressed.

> Exhausted, I sought
> a country inn, and found
> wisteria in bloom

⁓

At Hatsuse:

> One old man sits *zazen*
> in the corner of the temple
> on this spring night

Mangiku-maru wrote:

> Priests walk in high
> wooden clogs as rain falls through
> cherry blossoms

⁓

On Kazuraki Mountain:

> I still want to see
> in blossoms at dawn the face
> of the mountain god[51]

After visiting Mount Miwa and Mount Tafu, I crossed steep Hoso Pass:

> I climbed into air
> high above the skylarks—
> scaling a summit

At Dragon's Gate Waterfall:

> A bridge of flowers
> crossing Dragon's Gate would be
> my gift to drinkers

> Drinkers would be pleased
> to learn of a flower bridge
> crossing the waterfall

At Nijikō:

> The yellow rose
> petals—one by one—gone into
> roaring waterfalls

I visited other famous waterfalls—at Seirei, Furu, Nunobiki, and Minō—the last on my way to Kachio Temple.

On cherry blossoms:

> Mile after mile
> falls away each day I search
> for cherry blossoms

> Blossoming cherries,
> a gloomy sky, and, sadly,
> one arborvitae

> My fan for a cup,
> I drink from a downpour
> of cherry blossoms

I saw a beautiful clear stream pouring from a crack in a moss-covered stone:

> A fresh spring rain
> must have passed through all the leaves
> to nourish this spring

Throughout my three days in Yoshino, I enjoyed the opportunity to study cherry blossoms at various hours, predawn to dusk and past midnight when the moon was growing pale. I was too moved to write

even one poem, especially when my melancholy heart remembered fa-
mous poems by Saigyō and other ancient poets. All my lofty pretenses
and ambitions aside, my journey produced no poetry.

At Mount Kōya:

> A mountain pheasant cry
> fills me with fond longing for
> father and mother.

Mangiku-maru wrote:

> Embarrassed by
> cherry blossoms caught in my hair
> at the holy shrine

At Wakanoura:

> With spring departing,
> at Wakanoura Bay,
> I finally caught up

I wrote this haiku on the terrace at Kimii Temple, looking out at
the sea.

As my worn-out feet dragged me along, I was reminded of Saigyō and how much he suffered along the banks of Tenryū River. When I hired a horse, I remembered a famous priest who was humiliated when his horse threw him into a moat.

I was moved nonetheless by the beauty of the natural world, rarely seen mountain vistas and coastlines. I visited the temporary hermitages of ancient sages. Even better, I met people who had given over their whole lives to the search for truth in art. With no real home of my own, I wasn't interested in accumulating treasures. And since I traveled empty-handed, I didn't worry much about robbers.

I walked at a leisurely pace, preferring my walk even to riding a palanquin, eating my fill of coarse vegetables while refusing meat. My way turned on a whim since I had no set route to follow. My only concerns were whether I'd find suitable shelter for the night or how well straw sandals fit my feet. Each twist in the road brought new sights, each dawn renewed my inspiration. Wherever I met another person with even the least appreciation for artistic excellence, I was overcome with joy. Even those I'd expected to be stubbornly old-fashioned often proved to be good companions. People often say that the greatest pleasures of traveling are finding a sage hidden behind weeds or treasures hidden in trash, gold among discarded pottery. Whenever I encountered someone of genius, I wrote about it in order to tell my friends.

~

The spring day when one changes from heavy to lighter clothing:

> I shed a heavy coat
> for lighter clothes—and put it
> in my backpack

Mangiku-maru wrote:

> Once down from Yoshino
> Mountain, I sold my heavy
> padded cotton coat

While in Nara on the Buddha's birthday, I witnessed the birth of a fawn, a deeply moving experience:

> On Buddha's birthday
> a spotted fawn is born—
> just like that

The Chinese priest Ganjin, who founded Shōdai Temple and the Tendai sect, is said to have been blinded by sea salt during one of his seventy trials while on his journey to Japan. After deep bows at his statue, I wrote:

> With a new spring leaf,
> I'd be honored to wipe
> away your salty tears

Bidding farewell to an old friend in Nara:

> Like the buck's antlers,
> we point in slightly different
> directions, my friend

At the home of a friend in Osaka:

> Refreshed by talking
> about blooming irises
> along my journey

At Suma Beach:

> Moon-viewing, and yet—
> as though someone was missing—
> summer, Suma Beach[52]

> Seeing the hazy moon
> somehow was not quite enough—
> summer, Suma Beach

It was early summer when I walked along Suma Beach, thin clouds overhead, the moon particularly beautiful as nights grew shorter. The mountains were dark with new growth. Just as I thought it must be time to hear the first cuckoo, the eastern horizon began to glow and the hills around Ueno grew red and brown with wheat fields except where fishermen's huts dotted fields of white poppies.

> At dawn, the brown faces
> of fishermen emerge from
> fields of white poppies

The three villages on the beach were called East, West, and Central Suma, but none appeared to have any center of trade. An ancient poet attributed salt farms to Suma, but none remained. Small fish were drying on the sand, guarded from crows by villagers carrying bows and arrows. I wondered how people could resort to such cruelty without a pang of conscience, and remembered that Yoshitsune long ago won a bloody battle with the Heike clan in the mountains beyond the beach.

Deciding to visit the battle site, I started up Mount Tetsukai, but my young guide soon began trying to dissuade me. I bribed him with the promise of a feast. Barely sixteen, he looked much older than other village boys. He led the way, scrambling up a hundred feet of shale, slipping back, clinging to bamboo roots and weeds, huffing great breaths and soaking his clothes with sweat. It was only through his efforts that I reached the great Cloud Gate.

From the arrow tip
of a fisherman—the cry
of mountain cuckoo

A cuckoo's cry—
disappearing quickly
toward an island

Under a shade tree
at Suma Temple, I heard
a marching flute

I spent a night in Akashi:

> A trapped octopus—
> one night of dreaming
> with the summer moon

An ancient writer suggested autumn as the best time to visit. I found a deep sense of solitary loneliness in the landscape. And yet I would be a fool to think that by coming here in autumn I might have written better poetry. Such a thought only illustrates my poverty of imagination.

Awaji Island was just across the inlet. A small mountain on the mainland marked Suma Beach to the left, Akashi Beach to the right, reminding me of Tu Fu's description of a lake in China. But any more literate man would have thought of dozens of such scenes.

In the mountains above the beach, there was a tiny village that was the birthplace of two sisters whose unfortunate lives became the subject of the famous play, *Pine Winds*. Leaving the village, I took a narrow path winding up a ridge leading into Tamba Province, inching along cliffs with frightening names like Hell's Window and Headlong Fall.

At Ichi-no-tani, I looked down from the steep ridge where Yoshitsune led his forces in a great downhill charge, and saw the pine where he hung his war gong, and beyond it, across the valley, his enemy's campsite. Thinking of those tragic times, I imagined the old grandmother of the emperor taking him from his mother's shoulder, his legs caught in her robes as they fled to boats, the invading army at their heels. Court ladies ran with treasures wrapped in quilts—rare instruments and such—while other treasures were lost—imperial gifts for the fishes, makeup stands abandoned in sandy grass.

And that is why, even now, after a thousand years, the waves meet this shore with such a melancholy song.

SARASHINA TRAVELOGUE

AUTUMN WINDS FILLED MY HEART with a longing to see the full moon rising over Mount Obasute, a ragged peak where, in ancient times, Sarashina villagers abandoned their aging mothers to die among the stones. My haiku disciple, Etsujin, shared my desire, and we were joined by a servant sent by our friend Kakei.

The Kiso road was dangerous, winding over several steep mountain passes. Much as we tried to help one another, our inexperience showed. There were many mistakes. Nervous and worried, we made mistakes, but learning to laugh at them gave us courage to continue.

We met an old priest on the road, a man over sixty, carrying a crushing load on his bent back, and he wobbled breathlessly along with a stern, determined expression. My traveling companions, feeling compassion for him, lifted his burden from his shoulders and placed it on my horse, leaving me atop a large pile of gear. Mountains beyond mountains rose up over my head. To my left, a sheer cliff fell thousands of feet into a rushing river, leaving my stomach churning with every step of my horse. As we passed through Kakehashi, Nezame, and other dangerous places, the trail wound higher and higher until we were pushing our way through clouds. Dizzy from the height and teetering fearfully on my horse, I dismounted and walked on rubbery legs.

Then the servant mounted the horse, ignoring the danger. He began to doze off and nearly tumbled over a cliff. With every nod of his head, I was stricken with terror. Thinking it over, I realized that each of us is like the servant as we wade the shifting tides of this stormy world, blind to real danger. Even the Buddha watching from above would feel as I did for the servant.

—

At nightfall, we found a room in a poor priest's house. I lit a lamp and took out my ink stone and brush. Just as I was remembering the day's scenes and poems I composed along the way, the priest saw me touch my brow, and assumed I suffered travel fatigue. He insisted on recounting his own youthful travels along with parables from the sutras and miracles he had seen. Unfortunately, his interruption foiled my desire to write.

Just then, moonlight poured through leaves and cracks in the wall into a corner of the room. I heard villagers in the distance as they banged wooden clappers and shouted at deer to go away. My heart and mind felt the utter aloneness of autumn.

I suggested we have a drink in the moonlight, and our host quickly brought cups. Too large for refined tastes, they were trimmed with gaudy gold lacquer. City sophisticates wouldn't have touched them. But finding them in the back country, they pleased me. They were, I thought, more precious than the blue jeweled cups of the wealthy.

I'd sprinkle lacquer,
a decorative picture
on this hotel moon

Kakehashi Bridge—
even vines cling for their lives—
I cling like ivy

Kakehashi Bridge!
The first animals across—
ancient horse-trading days!

Etsujin wrote:

Midway across the bridge,
I hadn't courage to blink
as fog cleared away

A poem written on Mount Obasute:

Now I see her face,
the old woman, abandoned,
the moon her only companion

The sixteenth night moon!
I linger in Sarashina—
still in the country

Etsujin wrote:

In three days, I've seen
the bright moon three times in
a clear, cloudless sky

Slender, so slender
its stalk bends under dew—
little yellow flower

Piercing my tongue,
this daikon is spicy hot!
—an autumn wind

Kiso mountain chestnuts
will make a good souvenir
for city friends

Exchanging farewells,
departing, now I walk into
the Kiso autumn

A poem written at Zenkō Temple:

> Under bright moonlight,
> the four gates and the Four Sects
> are only one![53]

A storm blasts
Mount Asama, showering me
with windblown gravel

SELECTED HAIKU

It is New Year's Day
for each rice field's own sun—just
as each yearned for it

Ganjitsu wa
tagoto no hi koso
koishikere

Seeing the new year's
first flowers, I'll live seventy-
five years longer

Hatsu hana ni
inochi shichi-jū-
go-nen hodo

The new year's first snow—
how lucky to remain alone
at my hermitage

Hatsuyuki ya
saiwai an ni
makari aru

On New Year's Day,
each thought a loneliness as
autumn dusk descends

Ganjitsu ya
omoeba sabishi
aki no kure

It must be someone
else wearing this new kimono
this New Year morning

Tare yara ga
katachi ni nitari
kesa no haru

A new spring begins
the same old wealth—about
two quarts of rice

Haru tatsu ya
shinnen furuki
kome goshō

New Year's first snow—ah—
just barely enough to tilt
the daffodil

Hatsuyuki ya
suisen no ha no
tawamu made

Even the horse
catches my attention
this snowy morning

Uma wo sae
nagamura yuki no
ashita kana

My ears purified
by incense, now I can hear
the cuckoo's cry

Kiyoku kikan
mimi ni kō taite
hototogisu

Now spring has arrived
on a mountain with no name
in early morning haze

Haru nare ya
na mo naki yama no
asagasumi

You weren't home when I came—
even the plum blossoms were
in another yard

Rusu ni kite
ume sae yoso no
kakiho kana

Don't ever forget—
in the middle of the thicket,
blossoming plum

Wasuruna yo
yabu no naka naru
ume no hana

In every direction,
whatever greets the eye is
refreshingly cool

Ko no atari
me ni miyuru mono wa
mina suzushi

A pair of deer
groom each other hair by hair
with increasing care

Meoto jika ya
ke ni ke ga sorou te
ke mutsukashi

From what tree's
blossoming, I do not know,
but oh, its sweet scent!

Nan no ki no
hana towa shirazu
nioi kana

To blossoming cherries,
we recite Buddha's blessing
most gratefully

Yo ni sakaru
hana ni mo nebutsu
mōshi keri

With no ringing bell,
how does the village get by
on spring evenings?

Kane tsukanu
sato wa nami wo ka
haru no kure

Along my journey
through this temporal world, people
new-year-house-cleaning

Tabine shite
mishi ya ukiyo no
susu-harai

I still want to see
in blossoms at dawn the face
of the mountain god

Nao mi-tashi
hana ni ake yuku
kami no kao

This water's too cold—
you'll not get a moment's sleep,
Mr. Seagull

Mizu samuku
neiri kane taru
kamome kana

The bush warbler
in a grove of bamboo sprouts
sings of growing old

Uguisu ya
take no koyabu ni
oi wo naku

Among blossoming
peach trees everywhere,
the first cherry blooms

Saki midasu
mono no naka yori
hatsu-zakura

All hundred thousand
homes in Kyoto empty—
cherry blossom time

Kyō wa kuman
kusen kunju no
hana mi kana

Nesting white storks—
glimpsed through the leaves of
a blossoming cherry

Kō no su mo
mi raruru hana no
hagoshi kana

The old cherry tree's
final blossoms are her last
cherished memory

Ubazakura
saku ya rōgo no
omoi ide

Under a crescent moon
the fields grow hazy with
buckwheat flowers

Mikazuki ni
chi wa oboronari
soba no hana

The garden flowers,
without Mother at the house,
look awfully dreary

Unohana mo
haha naki yado zo
susamajiki

Flowers are best seen
by the eyes of poor people—
devilish thistle!

Hana wa shizu no
me ni mo mie keri
oni azami

It's altogether
fitting! —bean-floured rice balls
while blossom-hunting

Niawashi ya
mamenoko meshi ni
sakura gari

Between our two lives
there is also the life of
the cherry blossom

Inochi futatsu no
naka ni ikitaru
sakura kana

After morning snow
onion shoots rise in the garden
like little signposts

Kesa no yuki
nebuka o sono no
shiori kana

In this warm spring rain,
tiny leaves are sprouting
from the eggplant seed

Harusame ya
futaba ni moyuru
nasubi-dane

O departing spring,
with all the Ōmi people,
I'll miss you deeply

Yuku haru o
Ōmi no hito to
oshimi keru

Just one possession
in this lightly-lived life—
a gourd of rice

Mono hitotsu
waga yo wa karoki
hisago kana

Such a hangover!
Nothing to worry about,
with cherry blossoms

Futsuka-ei
monokawa hana no
aru aida

Plum blossom perfume!
It always recalls again
the vanishing cold

Mume ga ka ni
oi modosaruru
samusa kana

In windblown spring rain,
budding, like a straw raincoat,
a river willow

Harusame ya
mino fuki kaesu
kawa yanagi

Flitting butterflies
in the middle of a field—
sunlit shadows

Chō no tobu
bakari nonaka no
hikage kana

Old lazy-bones—
slowly roused from a nap by
falling spring rain

Bushōsa ya
kaki okosareshi
haru no ame

This spring scenery
has been properly prepared:
moon and plum blossoms

Haru mo yaya
keshiki totonou
tsuki to ume

Under full blossom—
a spirited monk and
a flirtatious wife

Sakari-ja hana ni
sozoro ukihōshi
numeri-zuma

Grass for a pillow,
the traveler knows best how
to see cherry blossoms

Kusamakura
makoto no hanami
shite mo koyo

From all these trees—
in salads, soups, everywhere—
cherry blossoms fall

Ko no moto ni
shiru mo namasu mo
sakura kana

Saigyō's hermitage
must be hidden somewhere in
this blossoming garden

Saigyō no
iori mo aran
hana no niwa

Saigyō's straw sandals
should be hung with honor from
this dewy pine

Saigyō no
waraji mo kakare
matsu no tsuyu

Just a cloud or two—
to rest the weary eyes
of the moon-viewer

Kumo oriori
hito wo yasumeru
tsukimi kana

A warbler singing—
somewhere beyond the willow,
before the thicket

Uguisu ya
yanagi no ushiro
yabu no mae

O bush warblers!
Now you've shit all over
my rice cake on the porch

Uguisu ya
mochi ni fun suru
en no saki

Within the skylark's song—
the distinct rhythm of
the pheasants' cry

Hibari naku
naka no hyōshi ya
kiji no koe

All day long, singing,
yet the day's not long enough
for the skylark's song

Nagaki hi wo
saezuri taranu
hibari kana

Sparrows from rice fields
flock to the tea plantation,
seeking refuge

Ina suzume
cha no ki batake ya
nige dokoro

Even among flowers,
sad to say, I can't open
my manuscript bag

Hana ni akanu
nageki ya kochi no
uta bukuro

A weathered temple,
blossoming peach, and, hulling rice,
just one old man

Furudera no
momo ni kome fumu
otoko kana

In a stiff spring breeze,
pipe clasped firmly in his mouth—
Mister Ferryman!

Harukaze ya
kiseru kuwaete
sendō-dono

Kannon's tiled temple
roof floats far away in clouds
of cherry blossoms

Kannon no
iraka miyari-tsu
hana no kumo

Blossoming cherries—
all week I've watched the crane
down from his mountain

Hana saki te
nanuka tsuru miru
fumoto kana

Clouds of cherry blossoms!
Is that temple bell in Ueno
or Asakusa?

Hana no kumo
kane wa Ueno ka
Asakusa ka

Down on the ground,
bowing to the very roots—
farewell to flowers

Chi ni taore
ne ni yori hana mo
wakare kana

Whenever winds blow,
the butterfly finds a new place
on the willow tree

Fuku tabi ni
chō no inaoru
yanagi kana

After heavy winds—
this morning, once again,
the peppers are crimson

Ōkaze no
ashita mo akashi
tōgarashi

Weather-beaten bones,
I'll leave your heart exposed
to cold, piercing winds

Nozarashi o
kokoro ni kaze no
shimu mi kana

The month's last night, moonless—
a thousand-year-old cedar
embraced by the storm

Misoka tsuki nashi
chitose ni sugi o
daku arashi

From an old plum tree
a mistletoe is growing—
blossoming plum

Ume no ki ni
nao yadorigi ya
ume no hana

At breaking sunrise,
glistening whitefish—an inch
of utter whiteness

Akebono ya
shirau shiroki
koto issun

Karasaki's pine,
compared to blossoming cherry,
looks a bit hazy

Karasaki no
mastu wa hana yori
oboro nite

A Dutchman arrives
to view cherry blossoms
from his saddle

Oranda mo
hana ni ki ni keri
uma ni kura

Things beyond number,
all somehow called to mind by
blossoming cherries

Samazama no
koto omoidasu
sakura kana

If my voice was good,
I'd sing a song of cherry
blossoms falling

Koe yokuba
utaō mono o
sakura chiru

Singing, planting rice,
village songs are more moving
than city poems

Satobito wa
ine ni uta yomu
miyako kana

Father and mother,
long gone, suddenly return
in the pheasant's cry

Chichi-haha no
shikiri ni koishi
kiji no koe

The baby sparrows
cry out, and in response, mice
answer from their nest

Suzume-go to
koe nakikawasu
nezumi no su

On a dark spring night,
a mysterious visitor
in the temple hall

Haru no yo ya
Komoridō yukashi
dō no sumi

The wandering crow
finds only plum blossoms
where its nest had been

Tabi garasu
furusu wa mume ni
nari ni keri

A lovely spring night
suddenly vanished while we
viewed cherry blossoms

Haru no yo wa
sakura ni akete
shinai keri

Steady spring rain
drains down through a wasp nest
to leak through the roof

Harusame ya
hachi no su tsutau
yane no mori

Spring passes
and the birds cry out—tears
in the eyes of fishes

Yuku haru ya
tori naki uo no
me wa namida

Culture's beginnings:
from the heart of the country
rice-planting songs

Furyu no
hajime ya oku no
ta ue uta

How very noble!
One who finds no satori
in the lightning flash

Inazuma ni
satoranu hito no
tōtosa yo

How foolish! In the dark
I grab a thorn, mistaking
it for a firefly

Gu ni kuraku
ibara o tsukamu
hotaru kana

So! Nothing at all happened!
Yesterday has vanished.
After blowfish soup.[54]

Ara nantomo na ya
kinō wa sugite
fukuto jiru

Morning glories
are such fine company
while eating breakfast!

Asagao ni
ware wa meshi kuu
otoko kana

Traveling this high
mountain trail, delighted
by wild violets

Yamaji kite
naniyara yukashi
sumiregusa

Hearing they eat snakes,
it's unnerving to listen
to the pheasant's cry

Hebi kuu to
kikeba osoroshi
kiji no koe

Live the lonely life!
Sing the Lonely Moon-Watcher's
songs of Nara

Wabi te sume
tsuki wabi sai ga
Nara cha-uta

The birdcatcher
discards his hat and rod—
taught by a cuckoo

Torisashi mo
kasa ya sute ken
hototogisu

Unloading its freight,
the camellia blossom bends,
spilling rainwater

Ochizama ni
mizu koboshikeri
hana tsubaki

This rabbit-ear iris
inspires me to compose
another haiku

Kakitsubata
ware ni hokku no
omoi ari

Falling willow leaves—
my master and I and
tolling temple bells

Chiru yanagi
aruji mo ware mo
kane wo kiku

Buried under moss
and ivy leaves, but from within
the tomb, a faint prayer

Koke uzumu
tsuta no utsutsu no
nebutsu kana

On a bare branch,
a solitary crow—
autumn evening

Kare eda ni
karasu no tomari keri
aki no kure

Out mushroom hunting—
dangerously close to caught in
late autumn showers

Takegari ya
abunaki koto ni
yūshigure

I've seen the provinces
and eight famous local scenes—
now Kehi's moon

Kuni guni no
hakkei sara ni
Kehi no tsuki

May this Shinto priest
sweep away my name—into
the River of Fallen Leaves

Miyamori yo
waga na o chirase
konohagawa

An aging peach tree—
don't strip and scatter its leaves,
cold autumn wind

Momo no ki no
sono ha chirasu na
aki no kaze

Old spider, what is
your song, how do you cry
in the autumn wind?

Kumo nani to
ne o nani to naku
aki no kaze

Snow fallen on snow,
and this evening, the full moon
of November

Yuki to yuki
koyoi shiwasu no
meigetsu ka

The housecat's lover
visits her frequently through
the burnt-out oven

Neko no tsuma
hetsui no kuzure yori
kayoi keri

At the ancient pond
a frog plunges into
the sound of water

Furuike ya
kawazu tobikomu
mizu no oto

This bright harvest moon
keeps me walking all night long
around the pond

Meigetsu ya
ike o meguri-te
yo mo sugara

For those who proclaim
they've grown weary of children,
there are no flowers

Ko ni aku to
mōsu hito ni wa
hana mo nashi

Now I see her face,
the old woman, abandoned,
the moon her only companion

Omokage ya
oba hitori naku
tsuki no tomo

Nothing in the cry
of cicadas suggests they
are about to die

Yagate shinu
keshiki wa miezu
semi no koe

Delight, then sorrow
afterward—aboard the
cormorant fishing boat

Omoshirōte
yagate kanashiki
ubune kana

Exhausted, I sought
a country inn, but found
wisteria in bloom

Kutabire-te
yado karu koro ya
fuji no hana

Among moon-gazers
at the ancient temple grounds
not one beautiful face

Tsukimi suru
za ni utsukushiki
kawo mo nashi

Intermittent rain—
no need at all to worry
over rice seedlings

Ame oriori
omou koto naki
sanae kana

A cuckoo cries,
and through a thicket of bamboo
the late moon shines

Hototogisu
otakeyabu wo
moru tsukiyo

Now a cuckoo's song
carries the haiku master
right out of this world

Hototogisu
ima wa haikaishi
naki yo kana

Over the brushwood door
the full moon—just as before—
as it was for Saigyō!

Shiba no to no
tsuki ya sono mama
Amida-bō

Seen in bright daylight,
its neck is burning red,
this little firefly!

Hiru mireba
kubisuji akaki
hotaru kana

Along the roadside,
blossoming wild roses
in my horse's mouth

Michi *no be no*
mukuge *wa uma ni*
kuwarekeri

The banana tree,
blown by winds, pours raindrops
into the bucket

Bashō *nowaki shite*
tarai *ni ame wo*
kiku *yo kana*

You, the butterfly;
me, Chuang Tzu—but who's which
in my dreaming heart?

Kimi *ya chō*
ware *ya Sōji ga*
yume *gokoro*

A butterfly—
how many times will it wing
over roof and wall?

Chō no hane
ikutabi koyuru
hei no yane

On a white poppy,
a butterfly's torn wing
is a keepsake

Shirageshi ni
hane mogu chō no
katami ka na

The horse turns his head—
from across the wide plain,
a cuckoo's cry

No wo yoko ni
uma hikimuke yo
hototogisu

Wrapping dumplings in
bamboo leaves, with one finger,
she tidies her hair

Chimaki yu
katate ni hasamu
hitai-gami

A trapped octopus—
one night of dreaming
with the summer moon

Takotsubo ya
hakanaki yume wo
natsu no tsuki

The bee emerging
from deep within the peony
departs reluctantly

Botan shibe fukaku
wakeizuru hachi no
nagori ka na

With a warbler for
a soul, it sleeps peacefully,
this mountain willow

Uguisu wo
tama ni nemuru ka
tao yanagi

That's my sake cup!
Don't come dropping mud in there,
nesting swallows!

Sakazuki ni
doro na otoshi so
mura tsubame

The morning glories
bloom, securing the gate
in my old fence

Asagao ya
hiru wa jō orosu
kado no kaki

From every direction
cherry blossom petals blow
into Lake Biwa

Shihō yori
hana fuki-irete
nio no umi

Long conversations
beside blooming irises—
joys of life on the road

Kakitsubata
gkataru mo tabi no
hitotsu kana

Old melon-grower—
I wish you could be with me
in this cool evening

Uri tsukuru
gkimi ga are na to
yūsuzumi

On Buddha's birthday
a spotted fawn is born—
just like that

Kambutsu no
hi ni umareau
kanoko kana

On Buddha's death day,
wrinkled tough old hands pray—
the prayer beads' sound

Nehan e ya
shiwade awasuru
juzu no oto

I slept at a temple—
and now with such seriousness
I watch the moon

Tera ni nete
makotogao naru
tsukimi kana

Behind Ise Shrine,
unseen, hidden by the fence,
Buddha enters Nirvana

Kami-gaki ya
omoi mo kakezu
nehan-zo

This ruined temple
should have its sad tale told only
by the clam digger

Kono yama no
kanashisa tsuge yo
tokoro-hori

As I applaud
with all the echoes—the dawn
of a summer moon

Te wo uteba
kodama ni akuru
natsu no tsuki

Even temple bells
seem to be ringing in
the cicada's cry

Tsuku kane mo
hibiku yō nari
semi no koe

I'd like to be drunk
and sleep among blooming pinks
on a cool stone

You te nen
nadeshiko sakeru
ishi no ue

It is still alive!
quivering in a frozen block,
little sea-slug!

Iki nagara
hitotsu ni kōru
namako kana

The young farm-child
interrupts rice husking to
gaze up at the moon

Shizu no ko ya
ine suri kakete
tsuki wo miru

The moon disappears
into darkening treetops
collecting the rain

Tsuki hayashi
kozue wa ame wo
mochi nagare

Now autumn begins,
the sea and all the fields
the same shade of green

Hatsu-aki ya
umi mo aota no
hito midori

A harvest moon,
and creeping up to my gate,
the rising tide

Meigetsu ya
kado ni sashi kuru
shiogashira

Under bright moonlight,
the four gates and the Four Sects
are only one!

Tsukikage ya
shimon shishū mo
tada hitotsu

Crossing half the sky
on my way to the capital,
big clouds promise snow

Kyō made wa
mada nakazora ya
yuki no kumo

Gray hairs being plucked,
and from below my pillow
a cricket singing

Shiraga nuku
makura no shita ya
kirigirisu

Searching storehouse eaves,
rapt in plum blossom smells,
the mosquito hums

Ka wo saguru
ume ni kura miru
nokiba kana

Drinking sake
brings on insomnia—
it snowed all night

Sake nomeba
itodo nerarenu
yoru no yuki

Crossing long fields,
frozen in its saddle,
my shadow creeps by

Samuki ta ya
bajō ni sukumu
kagebōshi

In my sickbed,
I can't even eat my rice cake—
blossoming peach

Wazuraeba
mochi o mo kuwazu
momo no hana

The morning glories
ignore our drinking party
and burst into bloom

Asagao wa
sakamori shiranu
sakari kana

Moonflower, evening-face—
just as I thrust my drunken
face out the window

Yūgao ya
yōte kao dasu
mado no ana

Old morning glory,
even you, as it turns out,
cannot be my friend

Asagao ya
kore mo mata waga
tomo narazu

A traveler's heart
is what you should emulate,
pasania bloom

Tabibito no
kokoro ni mo niyo
shii no hana

From the edge of death,
these chrysanthemums somehow
begin to blossom

Yase nagara
wari naki kiku no
tsubomi kana

In the herb garden,
I wonder which flowers to
use for my pillow

Yakuran ni
izure no hana o
kusamakura

At The Shallows,
the long-legged crane cool,
stepping in the sea

Shiogoshi ya
tsuru hagi nurete
umi suzushi

The cry of the dove
penetrates even the stone
door of this dark cave

Hato no koe
mi ni shimi wataru
iwato kana

Grass for a pillow,
the traveler knows best how
to see cherry blossoms

Kusamakura
makoto no hanami
shite mo ko yo

Chrysanthemums
blossom among stones in
the stonemason's garden

Kiku no hana
saku ya ishiya no
ishi no ai

Wake up! Wake up!
Then we'll become good friends,
sleeping butterfly

Okiyo okiyo
waga tomo ni sen
nuru kochō

In the old cow barn,
dusky sounds of mosquitoes—
summer heat lingers on

Ushibeya ni
ka no koe kuraki
zansho kana

In the fish market,
from among the little shrimps,
a cricket sings

Ama no ya wa
koebi ni majiru
itodo kana

Taking morning tea,
the monk remains in silence—
chrysanthemums bloom

Asa cha nomu
sō shizukanari
kiku no hana

Heavy falling mist—
Mount Fuji not visible,
but still intriguing

Kirishigure
fuji wo minu hi zo
omoshiroki

Lovely hermitage—
the moon, chrysanthemums, and
an acre of rice

Kakurega ya
tsuki to kiku to ni
ta san-tan

In this hermitage,
all the mosquitoes are small—
what a lovely gift!

Waga yado wa
ka no chiisaki o
chisō kana

A bush clover field—
provides a quiet night
for the mountain wolf

Hagi hara ya
hito yo wa yadose
yama no inu

Despite exhaustion
from my Kiso journey,
late moon viewing

Kiso no yase mo
mada naoranu ni
nochi no tsuki

Cold autumn wind
through a graveyard in Ise—
even more lonely

Aki no kaze
Ise no hakahara
nao sugoshi

A winter garden—
the moon also a thread,
like the insect's song

Fuyuniwa ya
tsuki mo ito naru
mushi no gin

With no umbrella
in cold, early winter rain—
ah, well! So be it!

Kasa mo naki
ware wo shigururu ka
nanto nanto

With no gods about,
waste and desolation reign
as dead leaves pile up

Rusu no ma ni
aretaru kami no
ochiba kana

Falling safely from
his horse into snow and sand,
rider drunk on wine

Yuki ya suna
muma yori ochiyo
sake no ei

These winter showers—
even the monkey searches
for a raincoat

Hatsu-shigure
saru mo komino wo
hoshige nari

On the coldest night,
we two sleeping together—
how comfortable!

Samu keredo
futari nuru yo zo
tanomoshiki

On Ancestors' Day,
the crematorium too
continues to smoke

Tama matsuri
kyō mo yakiba no
keburi kana

With clear melting dew,
I'd try to wash away the dust
of this floating world

Tsuyu toku-toku
kokoromi ni ukiyo
susuga-baya

Seas slowly darken
and the wild duck's plaintive cry
grows faintly white

Umi kurete
kamo no koe
honoka ni shiroshi

Lonely stillness—
a single cicada's cry
sinking into stone

Shizukasa ya
iwa ni shimi iru
semi no koe

Drawing purifying
water—like the monks' footsteps,
so clear and so cool

Mizutori ya
kōri no sō no
kutsu no oto

Ah, *matsutake*!
Its chafed, scarred skin looks just like
an actual pine

Matsutake ya
kabure ta hodo wa
matsu no nari

The oak's nobility—
indifferent to flowers—
or so it appears

Kashi no ki no
hana ni kamawanu
sugata kana

Normally spiteful—
but not even the crows
this snowy morning

Higoro nikuki
karasu mo yuki no
ashita kana

All the stones are dead,
the waters withered and gone—
winter and nothing

Ishi kare-te
mizu shibomeru ya
fuyu mo nashi

Awakened at midnight
by the sound of the rice jar
cracking from the ice

Kame waruru
yoru no kōri no
nezame kana

Even these long days
are not nearly long enough
for the skylarks' song

Nagaki hi mo
saezuri tara-nu
hibari kana

Chrysanthemums and
cockscomb—every flower gone
on Nichiren's death day

*Kiku keitō
kiri tsukushikeri
omeikō*

A wanderer,
so let that be my name—
the first winter rain

*Tabibito to
waga na yobare-n
hatsushigure*

All the field hands
enjoy a noontime nap after
the autumn moon

*Mina hito no
hirune no tane ya
aki no tsuki*

For all these people,
come, passing autumn shower,
no matter how cool

Hitobito wo
shigureyo yado wa
samuku tomo

Frosty, withering,
melancholy blossoming—
the final flowers

Shimo gare ni
saku wa shinki no
hana no kana

I'd sprinkle lacquer,
a decorative picture
on this hotel moon

Ano naka ni
maki-e kakitashi
yado no tsuki

Under one roof,
courtesans and monks asleep—
moon and bush clover

Hitotsuya ni
yūjo mo netari
hagi to tsuki

The end of autumn,
our future ripe with promise—
such green tangerines!

Yuku aki no
nao tanomoshi ya
aomikan

In the clear full moon
of late autumn, one can see
the New Year's beauty

Tsuki no kagami
koharu ni miru ya
me shōgatsu

Declining health—
a tooth finds a grain of sand
in the dried seaweed

Otoroi ya
ha ni kui ateshi
nori no suna

For today only,
we'll grow old together in
the first winter rain

Kyō bakari
hito mo toshiyore
hatsushigure

At the poor mountain temple,
the iron pot sounds like weeping
in the cold

Hinzan no
kama shimo ni naku
koe samushi

A salted sea bream—
its lips also look frozen—
at the seafood store

Shiodai no
haguki mo samushi
uo no tana

Fields half harvested,
cranes come wandering through—
a village autumn

Karikakeshi
tazura no tsuru ya
sato no aki

A potato leaf
awaits the harvest moon in
a burnt village field

Imo no ha ya
tsuki matsu sato no
yakibatake

It seems to me the
underworld would be like this—
late autumn evening

Gu anzuru ni
meido mo kaku ya
aki no kure

Winter seclusion—
propped once more against
this same worn post

Fuyugomori
mata yori sowan
kono hashira

A sad confluence—
everyone in the end turns into
young bamboo shoots

Uki fushi ya
takenoko to naru
hito no hate

Awaiting snowfall,
in the drinkers' faces,
lightning flashes

Yuki wo matsu
jōgo no kao ya
inabikari

Freshly reburnished,
the temple mirror is clear—
blossoming snowflakes

Togi naosu
kagami mo kiyoshi
yuki no hana

I would like to use
that scarecrow's tattered clothes
in this midnight frost

Karite nen
kakashi no sode ya
yowa no shimo

But for a woodpecker
tapping at a post, no sound
at all in the house

Kitsutsuki no
hashira wo tataku
sumai kana

Drunk from my hands,
icy spring water surprises
my aching teeth

Musubu yori
haya ha ni hibiku
izumi kana

Little river crab—
crawling up my leg while I soak
my feet in springwater.

Sazare gani
ashi hai noboru
shimizu kana

Those deep-rooted leeks
are washed so sparkling white—
utter coolness!

Nebuka shiroku
arai agetaru
samusa kana

Wet with morning dew
and splotched with mud, the melon
looks especially cool

Asatsuyu ni
yogorete suzushi
uri no tsuchi

Plates and rice bowls
grow faint in falling darkness—
the evening cools

Sarabachi mo
honokani yami no
yoisuzumi

Even in Kyoto,
how I long for old Kyoto
when the cuckoo sings

Kyō nite mo
Kyō natsukashi ya
hototogisu

A white chrysanthemum—
and to meet the viewer's eye,
not a mote of dust

Shiragiku no
me ni tatete miru
chiri mo nashi

Winter chrysanthemums
blanketed with fresh rice bran
beside the hand mill

Kangiku ya
konuka no kakaru
usu no hata

Being useless,
my daydreams are disturbed
by noisy warblers

Nōnashi no
nemutashi ware wo
gyōgyōshi

All along this road
not a single soul—only
autumn evening

Kono michi ya
yuku hito nashi ni
aki no kure

With my hair grown long
and my face turning ashen,
a sudden downpour

Kami hae te
yōgan aoshi
satsuki ame

After chrysanthemums,
but for daikon radishes,
there'll be nothing left

Kiku no nochi
daikon no hoka
sarani nashi

Autumn approaches
and the heart begins to dream
of four-tatami rooms

Aki chikaki
kokoro no yoru ya
yojōhan

Why just this autumn
have I grown suddenly old—
a bird in the clouds

Kono aki wa
nande toshiyoru
kumo ni tori

A lightning flash!
Where peoples' faces were,
only a pampas blade

Inazuma ya
kao no tokoro ga
susuki no ho

A lightning flash—
and, piercing the darkness,
the night heron's cry

Inazuma ya
yami no kata yuku
goi no koe

A hundred years!
All here in the garden in
these fallen leaves

Momotose no
keshiki wo niwa no
ochiba kana

Rested from your journey,
now you'll understand my haiku,
old autumn wind

Tabineshite
waga ku o shire ya
aki no kaze

Weary of travel,
how many days like this?
The winds of autumn

Tabi ni akite
kyō ikuka yara
aki ni kaze

Tremble, oh my grave—
in time my cries will be
only this autumn wind

Tsuka mo ugoke
waga naku koe wa
aki no kaze

Already sorrowful,
now you add loneliness too,
old autumn temple

Uki ware wo
sabishi garase yo
aki no tera

A rolling cloud—like
a dog pissing on the run—
dense winter showers

Yuku kumo ya
inu no kake-bari
murashigure

A snowy morning—
sitting alone with dried salmon,
enjoying chewing

Yuki no asa
hitori kara-zake o
kami-e-tari

Year-end housekeeping—
hanging his own shelf at last,
the carpenter

Susuhaki wa
ono ga tana tsuru
daiku kana

In clear moonlight,
because he fears the fox, I go
with my lover-boy

Tsuki sumu ya
kitsune kowagaru
chigo no tomo

Feline love's like that—
afterward, back in its bed,
hazy moonlight

Neko no koi
yamu toki neya no
oborozuki

Has this harvest moon
suddenly burst into bloom
in the cotton field?

Meigetsu no
hana ka to miete
watabatake

Only ears of wheat
to cling to as I pause
for a parting word

Mugi no ho wo
chikara ni tsukamu
wakare kana

Your song caresses
the depths of loneliness,
high mountain bird

Uki ware wo
sabishi garase yo
kankodori

In this late autumn,
my next-door neighbor—
how does he get by?

Aki fukaki
tonari wa nani wo
suru hito zo

Fanning steaming rice,
his wife prepares a simple feast—
cool evening air

Meshi augu
kaka ga chisō ya
yūsuzumi

The whole household—
each with white hair and cane—
visiting a grave

Ie wa mina
tsue ni shiraga no
hakamairi

A little cuckoo—
its stark cry stretches clear
across the water

Hototogisu
koe yokotau ya
mizu no ue

With plum blossom scent,
this morning sun emerges
along a mountain trail

Mume ga ka ni
notto hi no deru
yamaji kana

On Suruga Road,
the orange blossoms also
have tea's odor

Surugaji ya
hana tachibana mo
cha no nioi

Fragrant chrysanthemums—
in Nara, there are many
friendly old buddhas

Kiku no ka ya
Nara ni wa furuki
hotoke tachi

A samurai party—
pungent as daikon radish,
their conversation!

Mononofu no
daikon nigaki
hanashi kana

Sweeping the garden,
forget all about snow!
A household broom

Niwa hakite
yuki wo wasururu
hahaki kana

Every New Year Day—
again the monkey wears
a monkey mask

Toshidoshi ya
saru ni kisetaru
saru no men

Even the whitefish
opens black eyes to the law
of Buddha's net

Shirauo ya
kuroki me wo aku
nori no ami

Somehow not yet dead
at the end of my journey—
this autumn evening

Shini mo se nu
tabine no hate yo
aki no kure

Mourning the Death of Ranran[55]

In cold autumn wind,
sadly it is broken—my
mulberry walking stick

Akikaze ni
orete kanashiki
kuwa no tsue

On a Portrait of Hotei, God of Good Fortune

How much I desire!
Inside my little satchel,
the moon and flowers

Monohoshi ya
fukuro no uchi no
tsuki to hana

Bashō's Death Poem

Sick on my journey,
only my dreams will wander
these desolate moors

Tabi ni yande
yume wa kareno wo
kakemeguru

AFTERWORD

Bashō arrived in his hometown of Ueno in November 1689, exhausted by his travels and weakened by failing health. But after a couple of months, he once again took to the road accompanied by a friend, Rotsū, this time to see the famous Shinto festival at Kasuga Shrine in Nara in early January of 1690. By early February, he was in Kyoto to visit his friend Kyorai, and from there went to the village of Zeze, on the shore of Lake Biwa, where he was welcomed by a throng of students on New Year's Day (February 9 on the lunar calendar). Bashō left Rotsū there a few days later and returned alone to Ueno, where he spent the next three months being feted and attending haiku gatherings.

It was during this stay in Ueno that he first began to advocate the poetic principle of *karumi*, "lightness," urging his followers to "seek beauty in plain, simple, artless language" by observing ordinary things very closely. *Karumi*, together with existential Zen loneliness (*sabi*) and elegantly understated, unpretentious natural beauty (*shibumi*), characterize his final work. His life had been profoundly shaped by *wabi*, a principle as much moral as aesthetic, and which suggests a spiritual prosperity achieved through material poverty together with a deep appreciation of things old, worn, modest, and simple. These last years, he wrote at the height of his powers, a lifetime of devoted study bringing him full circle, back to the most simple, least consciously artful poetry imaginable.

Around the first of May, he returned to Zeze, where his students had refurbished a tiny mountain cottage, naming it Genjū-an, the Phantom Hut, in his honor. From his hillside behind Ishiyama Temple, he enjoyed a panoramic view of Lake Biwa and the Seta River. Except for a ten-day visit with Kyorai in Kyoto, he rarely left his retreat over the next four months. Near the end of his stay, he wrote a short prose meditation, *Genjū-an-no-ki*, in which he concludes, "In the end, without skill or talent, I've given myself over entirely to poetry. Po Chu-i labored at it until he nearly burst. Tu Fu starved rather than abandon it. Neither my intelligence nor my writing is comparable to such men. Nevertheless, in the end, we *all* live in phantom huts."

Near the end of August 1690, he moved a little farther up the shore to another cottage, located on the grounds of another Buddhist temple, perhaps because his health was once again failing, and this one brought him closer to his students who might need to care for him. He stayed there until late October, when he returned once again to Ueno.

As his health improved, he made several trips to Kyoto and participated in a number of haiku gatherings. In the late spring of 1691, he moved into a cottage in Kyoto that Kyorai had prepared for him, and there, during the month of May, he composed that last of his *haibun*, *Saga nikki* (*Saga Diary*). But he was rarely alone there, and often in the company of Kyorai and another colleague, Bonchō, who were busy editing the haiku anthology *Sarumino* (*The Monkey's Raincoat*), and were constantly seeking his advice. He spent a month at Bonchō's house.

On July 20, 1691, he moved into a new cottage on the grounds of Gichū Temple, near the Genjū Hut where he'd been the previous year. His new cottage, Mumyō-an, Nameless Hut, quickly became his favorite. He was especially fond of looking out on the mountains and fields of the Iga Basin:

Under the harvest moon,
fog rolling down from foothills,
mist and clouds in the fields

Meigetsu ni
fumoto no kiri ya
ta no kumori

His poem plays with a pillow word or fixed epithet, "clouds and rain," often used to allude to sexual union in classical Japanese and Chinese poetry. It's a faint but profound allusion to the eroticism of the fields and the food they produce. Typical of late Bashō, he begins and ends in simple objective description, behind which lies a wealth of evocation.

On his deathbed three years later, dictating his will, he asked to be buried at Mumyō-an. He remained there until late November, when he finally felt strong enough to make the return trip to Edo. He had been gone two and a half years.

When he arrived in Edo a month later in the company of his traveling companions, he moved into a house in the Nihonbashi district, having given up his cottage in Fukagawa at the beginning of his journey north. In a prose introduction to haiku written upon his return, he says, "Having no real place of my own, I have traveled for six or seven years and suffered from many ailments. Memories of old friends and disciples and their warm hospitality drew me back to Edo." But all was not tranquil. Bashō fell out with several former disciples who had succumbed to ambition. He scolded one in the opening haiku of a linked verse:

> It should have remained green.
> So why has it changed color,
> this red pepper?

> *Aokute mo*
> *aru beki mono wo*
> *tōgarashi*

He wrote to a friend in Zeze in the spring of 1692, complaining, "Everywhere in this city I see people writing poetry to try to win prizes or notoriety. You can imagine what they write. Anything I might say to them would no doubt end in harsh words, so I pretend not to hear or see them." He skipped his customary spring cherry-blossom viewing, saying bitterly, "All the famous cherry blossom sites are overrun with noisy, ambitious seekers after fame." Once again, he considered abandoning the world of poetry, writing, "I tried to give up the Way of Elegance (*fūga-no-michi*) and stop writing poems, but something always stirred my heart and mind—such is its magic."

In May 1692, friends and disciples under the direction of Sora and Bashō's former patron, Sampu, completed construction of the third Bashō-an at the mouth of the Sumida River, and the poet moved in. He participated in a few select haiku gatherings over the following months, and welcomed several friends from distant places where he had journeyed. By the end of the year, he was busy with students and social responsibilities once again, complaining that he could find no peace.

By this time, the poet's nephew, Tōin, was dying of tuberculosis, and Bashō provided a home for him, borrowing money to pay for his care. He was also caring for a woman named Jutei and her three children, although their relationship is unclear. She may have been Bashō's mistress years earlier, before becoming a nun. It seems clear that Bashō was not the father of her children, leading some scholars to speculate that she was the wife of Tōin. In any case, the poet borrowed again to care for her and her children. Tōin died at Bashō-an in the spring of 1693. Jutei moved into Bashō-an in early 1694, shortly after the poet returned to Ueno, and she died there in midsummer.

Bashō fell into a deep depression following Tōin's death. He complained of "too much useless chatter" among his visitors, but was forced to participate in haiku gatherings in order to pay bills. He sweltered and again suffered terrible headaches and fever all summer until August, when he closed and bolted his gate, refusing to see anyone. He remained a hermit for the following two months before gradually reemerging for literary gatherings as his health improved and his depression began to lift.

By early 1694, Bashō was overcome by wanderlust again. On the one hand, he longed to journey southwest to visit Shikoku and Kyushu on a major adventure like his northern trip; on the other hand, as he observed in a letter, he felt he was nearing the end. He planned to depart in April, but his plans were postponed week by week because he suffered once again from chills and fever and migraine headaches.

Finally, on June 3, the weakened poet was placed on a litter by Jutei's son, Jirōbei, and Sora, and they departed, leaving Bashō-an to the dying nun and her two daughters. Jirōbei and Bashō arrived in Nagoya nearly two weeks later, their journey made ever more difficult by traveling during the rainy season. After a night of celebration and two days recovering their strength, they moved on to Ueno. Bashō was pleased to be celebrated in his hometown, but was far too weak to participate in any festivities. His chills, fever, and headaches per-sisted.

After a couple of weeks, the poet feeling a little stronger, they visited the Ōtsu area again, then moved on to Kyoto, where Bashō spent most of a month visiting with his students and writing linked verse, always advocating on behalf of *karumi*. He believed that poetry should arise naturally from close observation, revealing itself in the careful use of ordinary language. Still weakened, he was nevertheless in good spirits despite being constantly pressured to meet social re-sponsibilities.

Upon learning of the death of his mother, Jirōbei returned to Edo. Bashō returned to his cherished Nameless Hut on the southern shore of Lake Biwa. It was likely at the Mumyō Hut that he made his last revisions of *Narrow Road to the Interior*, the manuscript of which he had carried through his many journeys, editing, revising, and polishing as he went. Near the end of August, he visited Kyoto again before moving into a new cottage built by his students behind his elder brother's house in Ueno. He moved in just in time to host a harvest moon viewing party.

Several weeks later, Jirōbei returned from Edo. The two were joined by Bashō's nephew and a couple of students, and the party of five set out for Osaka at the urging of more Bashō followers there. They made a brief stay in Nara to enjoy a chrysanthemum festival along the way. Despite being overcome by persistent fever, chills, and headaches once again on the very evening of their arrival in Osaka, the poet felt obliged to attend festivities in his honor. He was exhausted.

Weakened by his recurring fever, he struggled for a week just to maintain himself, and his condition improved somewhat by the second week of November. But by the middle of the month, his exhausted body was ravaged by diarrhea. He became severely dehydrated. He grew increasingly emaciated. He stopped eating altogether, and dictated his will. He gathered all his strength to write a brief note to his brother, then asked students to write him a final verse, warning them against expecting advice "on even as much as one word." He also asked them to burn incense. "Your teacher is gone," he told them.

Bashō's longtime friend Kyorai asked about the master's *jisei* (death poem), and was told, "Tell anyone who asks that all of my everyday poems are my *jisei*."

Sick on my journey,
only my dreams will wander
these desolate moors

Tabi ni yande
yume wa kareno wo
kakemeguru

Kyorai wanted to know whether "Tabi ni yande" should be considered the master's death poem. Bashō replied, "It was written in my sickness, but it is not my *jisei*. Still, it can't be said that it's *not* my death poem either." He had summoned a student and dictated the poem well after midnight just a few days earlier, promising, "This will be my last obsession."

But once again he succumbed to the magic of *fūga-no-michi*, writing a last poem:

A white chrysanthemum—
and to meet the viewer's eye,
not a mote of dust

Shiragiku no
me ni tatete miru
chiri mo nashi

The second line is lifted entirely from a famous poem by Saigyō. He tried several poems using "chiri mo nashi," and it remains uncertain whether this was his final version. That dust mote, present or not, moves back beyond Saigyō to recall the teachings of the earliest Ch'an masters. The dust mote on the mirror is the foundation of a famous koan. At the end, Bashō remained as he began: a follower, not an imitator, of the great tradition of Japanese and Chinese Zen poetry. The whole tradition is brought to bear in the utterly clear, simple language of his poem: elegant simplicity.

Bashō was visited by his oldest follower and friend, Kikaku, but was too weak to say much of anything. He slept for hours. The following day, he awoke to flies buzzing around his screen, and laughed, "Those flies *like* having a sick man around." They proved to be his last words. In the afternoon, he slept again, breathing his last at 4:00 PM.

The next day, his body was carried back to Mumyō-an at Gichū-ji, where he was buried.

His fundamental teaching remained his conviction that in composing a poem, "There are two ways: one is entirely natural, in which the poem is born from within itself; the other way is to make it through the mastery of technique." His notion of the poem being "born within itself" should under no circumstances be confused with its being self-originating. A fundamental tenet of Buddhism runs exactly to the contrary: nothing is self-originating. Bashō's poems were in fact a natural product of his close observation of the natural *relationships* of people and things, our presence in "nature." He prized sincerity and clarity and instructed, "Follow nature, return to nature, be nature." He had learned to meet each day with fresh eyes. "Yesterday's self is already worn out!"

Another of his last poems might serve equally well as his *jisei:*

All along this road
not a single soul—only
autumn evening

Kono michi ya
yaku hito nashi ni
aki no kure

The "road" or path of this poem is as much aesthetic and metaphysical as literal. Bashō's *kadō,* or Way of Poetry, is singular. The "autumn" of the poem is as much the autumn of his life as it is a season. His is the aloneness of everyday *kenshō,* daily enlightenment, and of all who live and practice the arts of Zen, the arts of the Tao, following the Way of Poetry.

NOTES

1. This line echoes the famous preface to a poem ("Peach Garden Banquet on a Spring Night") by the T'ang dynasty poet Li Po.
2. Bashō is thinking here of the T'ang poet Tu Fu (712–770) and the wandering monk Saigyō (1118–1190).
3. "Doll's House" refers to Hina Matsuri, Girls' Festival, comparing his tiny thatched hut to his patron's mansion.
4. This is an allusion to *The Tale of Genji*.
5. Go refers to the ancient Chinese board game played with black and white "stones."
6. Konoshiro (literally, "In-place-of-child") refers to another similar legend.
7. Kūkai, also called Kōbō Daishi (774–835), founded the Shingon Buddhist sect. The temple at Nikkō was actually founded by Shōdō (737–817).
8. Japanese poets often changed their names, as had Bashō himself. Traveling in Buddhist robes was both safer and in keeping with Bashō's spiritual pilgrimage.
9. This refers to the Shinto and Buddhist spring-bathing ritual.
10. Bashō is referring to the story in the Noh play *Sessho-seki*, which is named after this stone.

11. This legendary feat is told in *The Tale of the Heike*.

12. This refers to the "rain clogs" of En-no-Gyōja, eighth-century founder of the Shūgen sect of Buddhism.

13. Bashō studied Zen under Butchō (1643–1715) at Chokei Temple in Edo between 1673 and 1684.

14. Myozenji and Houn are Chinese Zen (Ch'an) masters famed for their asceticism.

15. Saigyō (1118–1190) was one of the most influential early Buddhist recluse-poets.

16. This poem echoes a famous poem by Saigyō in the *Shinkokinshū*.

17. Bashō is referring here to poems by Noin and Yorimasa, both influences on Saigyō.

18. Kiyosuke (1104–1177) was a Heian period poet.

19. Gyōki (668–749) was high priest during the Nara period and was known as a bodhisattva.

20. Minamoto Yoshitsune (1159–1189) was the military leader for the Genji clan and celebrated in stories in *Tale of the Heike* and various Noh plays.

21. Benkei (fl. twelfth century) was a follower of Yoshitsune.

22. Tenjin Shrine honors Sugiwara Michizane (835–903), who was exiled in life, and then deified as Tenjin, the "god of letters."

23. Ungo Zenji (1583–1659) was a well-known monk of his day.

24. Kembutsu was a famous twelfth-century priest Saigyō visited in Matsushima.

25. Bashō's poem is also inspired in part by a poem of Saigyō's, written at the gravesite of the poet Fujiwara Sanekata, who died in exile in 998:

    He left us nothing
    but his own eternal name—
    just that final stroke.
    On his poor grave on the moor,
    one sees only pampas grass

26. Kanefusa (1127–1189), although old at the time, fought alongside Yoshitsune.

27. Bashō here mentions Sennin (The Hall of the Immortals) almost as a prayer for longevity.

28. See the *Li Chi* or Confucian *Book of Rites*: "A sweet wind from the South" indicates warmth and clarity.

29. Gyōson Sōjō was a poet-priest whose work Bashō was familiar with from the *Kinyoshū*.

30. This image alludes to famous poems by Wang Wei and Tu Fu.

31. Tanabata Matsuri celebrates the annual romantic reunion of lovers separated all but one night per year, when they are said to cross a bridge of magpies on the seventh night of the seventh month. See also *The Diary of Izumi Shikibu*.

32. Sado Island was home of political exiles. The "River of Heaven" is the Milky Way.

33. Sanemori's tale is told in *Tale of the Heike*, in *Igenpei Seisuki*, and in a Noh play by Zeami called *Sanemori*.

34. Teitoku (1571–1653) was a scholar of haiku and *renga* who lived in Kyoto.

35. The image of the parting of paired geese recalls a poem of Bashō's written while still in his teens following the death of his lord, Sengin; it also carries echoes of Tu Fu's poetry.

36. It was a custom for travelers to wear inscribed hatbands saying they traveled "with the Buddha," both for good luck and to reduce the likelihood of robbery and other risks of travel.

37. See *Chuang Tzu*, chapter 8.

38. Dōgen (1200–1253) was founder of the Sōtō Zen sect.

39. Ise is Japan's principal Shinto shrine.

40. This line is by Ch'an (Zen) monk Kuang-wen (1127–1279) from a poem no doubt inspired in part by Chuang Tzu.

41. Tu Mu (803–852) was one of the many great poets of the T'ang dynasty. The poem Bashō refers to reads "My quirt dangling freely, I trust my horse. / Traveling miles without a cock crow, / I doze off, passing through the woods, / but wake with a start when leaves fly."

42. Urashima Tarō was a mythical fisherman who returned to his village following three hundred years in the company of a sea goddess. Disobeying her instruction not to look into a small jeweled box, his age suddenly overcame him.

43. See *Chuang Tzu*, chapter 1, for the Taoist sage's remarks on the usefulness of a "useless" tree.

44. Po-i (dates unknown) was an advisor to the court during the Chou dynasty; when his advice was ignored, he became a famous recluse. Hsu

Yu was a renowned hermit who, when Emperor Yao offered him his kingdom, "washed out his ears and fled civilization."

45. Lady Tokiwa was the concubine of Yoshitomo (1123–1160) who led a rebellion against his father, Tameyoshi, head of the powerful Minamoto warrior clan. Yoshitomo was eventually murdered while traveling alone following a lost battle. Lady Tokiwa is thought to have been murdered by robbers, also while traveling alone.

46. Chikusai was a comic folk hero who wandered the land practicing goofy quackery and reciting verse.

47. The Water Drawing Ceremony is performed during the second month; the service includes monks walking meditation around the inner sanctuary.

48. Bashō is here drawing a comparison between his host and the Sung dynasty poet Lin He-ching, the "poet of cranes and plum blossoms."

49. It was—and in rural Japan, still is—the custom to save an infant's umbilical cord, keeping it with birth records.

50. Bashō was visiting the ruins of a famous temple built in the eighth century on Bōdai (Buddhahood) Mountain.

51. On Kazuraki Mountain there is a shrine to the Shinto deity Hitokotonushi, famous for his ugly face, which he tried to keep hidden from people.

52. Suma was the site of a fierce battle between the Genji and Heike clans in the twelfth century.

53. The Four Sects of Buddhism are Tendai, Jōdo, Ji, and Zen.

54. Blowfish, unless cleaned and cooked properly, can be fatally poisonous.

55. Matsukura Ranran (1647–1693) was one of Bashō's first disciples in Edo. Three years before his death, he resigned his post as a samurai to devote his life to poetry. Ranran was "mulberry age" (forty-six or forty-seven) when he died.

BIBLIOGRAPHY

Bashō in English:

Aitken, Robert. *A Zen Wave*. Weatherhill, 1978.

Britton, Dorothy. *A Haiku Journey*. Kodansha, 1974. A translation of *Oku no hosomichi*.

Blyth, R. H., *Haiku* (four volumes). Hokuseido Press, 1949–50.

———. *A History of Haiku* (two volumes). Hokuseido Press, 1963–4.

Corman, Cid, and Kamaike Susumu. *Back Roads to Far Towns*. Grossman, 1968. A translation of *Oku no hosomichi*.

Keene, Donald. *The Narrow Road to Oku*. Kodansha, 1996.

McCullough, Helen Craig. *Classical Japanese Prose*. Stanford University Press, 1990. Includes translations of *Oku no hosomichi* and *Nozarashi Kikō*.

Miner, Earl and Hiroko Odagiri. *The Monkey's Straw Raincoat*. Princeton University Press, 1981. A translation of *Sarumino* and several other linked verses from the Bashō School.

Oseko, Toshiharu. *Bashō's Haiku* (two volumes). Maruzen, 1990.

Sato, Hiroaki. *Bashō's Narrow Road*. Stone Bridge Press, 1996.

Shirane, Haruo. *Traces of Dreams: Landscape, Cultural Memory and the Poetry of Bashō*. Stanford University Press, 1998. A critical study.

Ueda, Makoto. *Matsuo Bashō*. Twayne World Authors Series, 1970. An introductory critical biography.

Ueda, Makoto. *Bashō and His Interpreters*. Stanford University Press, 1992.

Yuasa, Noboyuki. *The Narrow Road to the Deep North and Other Travel Sketches*. Penguin, 1966.

ABOUT THE TRANSLATOR

Sam Hamill is the author of more than thirty books of poetry, essays, and translations from the classical Chinese and Japanese, ancient Greek, Latin, and other languages. He has been a recipient of fellowships from the Woodrow Wilson Foundation, the Andrew Mellon Foundation, the National Endowment for the Arts, the Guggenheim Foundation, and the Japan-U.S. Friendship Commission. He lives near Port Townsend, Washington.

SHAMBHALA CLASSICS

Appreciate Your Life: The Essence of Zen Practice, by Taizan Maezumi Roshi.

The Art of Peace, by Morihei Ueshiba. Edited by John Stevens.

The Art of War, by Sun Tzu. Translated by the Denma Translation Group.

The Art of Worldly Wisdom, by Baltasar Gracián. Translated by Joseph Jacobs.

Awakening to the Tao, by Liu I-ming. Translated by Thomas Cleary.

Bodhisattva of Compassion: The Mystical Tradition of Kuan Yin, by John Blofeld.

The Book of Five Rings, by Miyamoto Musashi. Translated by Thomas Cleary.

The Book of Tea, by Kakuzo Okakura.

Breath by Breath: The Liberating Practice of Insight Meditation, by Larry Rosenberg.

Cutting Through Spiritual Materialism, by Chögyam Trungpa.

The Diamond Sutra and The Sutra of Hui-neng, translated by Wong Mou-lam and A. F. Price.

The Essential Teachings of Zen Master Hakuin, translated by Norman Waddell.

For the Benefit of All Beings, by H.H. the Dalai Lama. Translated by the Padmakara Translation Group.

The Great Path of Awakening, by Jamgön Kongtrül. Translated by Ken McLeod.

Insight Meditation: A Psychology of Freedom, by Joseph Goldstein.

The Japanese Art of War: Understanding the Culture of Strategy, by Thomas Cleary.

Kabbalah: The Way of the Jewish Mystic, by Perle Epstein.

Lovingkindness: The Revolutionary Art of Happiness, by Sharon Salzberg.

Meditations, by J. Krishnamurti.

Monkey: A Journey to the West, by David Kherdian.

The Myth of Freedom and the Way of Meditation, by Chögyam Trungpa.

Narrow Road to the Interior: And Other Writings, by Matsuo Bashō. Translated by Sam Hamill.

The Places That Scare You: A Guide to Fearlessness in Difficult Times, by Pema Chödrön.

The Rumi Collection: An Anthology of Translations of Mevlâna Jalâluddin Rumi, edited by Kabir Helminski.

Seeking the Heart of Wisdom: The Path of Insight Meditation, by Joseph Goldstein and Jack Kornfield.

Seven Taoist Masters: A Folk Novel of China, translated by Eva Wong.

Shambhala: The Sacred Path of the Warrior, by Chögyam Trungpa.

Siddhartha, by Hermann Hesse. Translated by Sherab Chödzin Kohn.

The Spiritual Teaching of Ramana Maharshi, by Ramana Maharshi.

Start Where You Are: A Guide to Compassionate Living, by Pema Chödrön.

T'ai Chi Classics, translated with commentary by Waysun Liao.

Tao Teh Ching, by Lao Tzu. Translated by John C. H. Wu.

The Taoist I Ching, by Liu I-ming. Translated by Thomas Cleary.

The Tibetan Book of the Dead: The Great Liberation through Hearing in the Bardo, translated with commentary by Francesca Fremantle and Chögyam Trungpa.

Training the Mind and Cultivating Loving-Kindness, by Chögyam Trungpa.

The Tree of Yoga, by B. K. S. Iyengar.

The Way of a Pilgrim and The Pilgrim Continues His Way. Translated by Olga Savin.

The Way of the Bodhisattva, by Shantideva. Translated by the Padmakara Translation Group.

For a complete list, please visit www.shambhala.com.